THE BIBLE *in a*
DISENCHANTED AGE

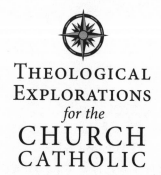

THEOLOGICAL
EXPLORATIONS
for the
CHURCH
CATHOLIC

THE BIBLE *in a* DISENCHANTED AGE

✳ ✦ ✳ ✦ ✳ ✦ ✳ ✦ ✳

THE ENDURING POSSIBILITY OF CHRISTIAN FAITH

R. W. L. Moberly

𝕭

Baker Academic

a division of Baker Publishing Group
Grand Rapids, Michigan

Published by Baker Academic
a division of Baker Publishing Group
P.O. Box 6287, Grand Rapids, MI 49516-6287
www.bakeracademic.com

Printed in the United States of America

Library of Congress Cataloging-in-Publication Data
Names: Moberly, R. W. L., author.
Title: The Bible in a disenchanted age : the enduring possibility of Christian faith / R. W. L. Moberly.
Description: Grand Rapids : Baker Academic, 2018. | Series: Theological explorations for the Church Catholic | Includes bibliographical references and index.
Identifiers: LCCN 2017028469 | ISBN 9780801099519 (cloth : alk. paper)
Subjects: LCSH: Bible—Criticism, interpretation, etc. | Bible—Hermeneutics.
Classification: LCC BS511.3 .M63 2018 | DDC 220.6—dc23
LC record available at https://lccn.loc.gov/2017028469

18   19   20   21   22   23   24   7   6   5   4   3   2   1

For John-Paul and Rachel

CONTENTS

SERIES PREFACE

Long before Brian McLaren began speaking about a "generous orthodoxy," John Wesley attempted to carry out his ministry and engage in theological conversations with what he called a "catholic spirit." Although he tried to remain "united by the tenderest and closest ties to one particular congregation"[1] (i.e., Anglicanism) all his life, he also made it clear that he was committed to the orthodox Christianity of the ancient creeds, and his library included books from a variety of theological traditions within the church catholic. We at Nazarene Theological Seminary (NTS) remain committed to the theological tradition associated with Wesley but, like Wesley himself, are very conscious of the generous gifts we have received from a variety of theological traditions. One specific place this happens in the ongoing life of our community is in the public lectures funded by the generosity of various donors. It is from those lectures that the contributions to this series arise.

---

1. John Wesley, *Sermon 39*, "Catholic Spirit," §III.4, in *Bicentennial Edition of the Works of John Wesley* (Nashville: Abingdon, 1985), 2:79–95. We know, however, that his public ties with Anglicanism were at some points in his life anything but tender and close.

The books in this series are expanded forms of public lectures presented at NTS as installments in two ongoing, endowed lectureships: the Earle Lectures on Biblical Literature and the Grider-Winget Lectures in Theology. The Earle Lecture series is named in honor of the first professor of New Testament at NTS, Ralph Earle. Initiated in 1949 with W. F. Albright for the purpose of "stimulating further research in biblical literature," this series has brought outstanding biblical scholars to NTS, including F. F. Bruce, I. Howard Marshall, Walter Brueggemann, and Richard Hays. The Grider-Winget Lecture series is named in honor of J. Kenneth Grider, longtime professor of theology at NTS, and in memory of Dr. Wilfred L. Winget, a student of Dr. Grider and the son of Mabel Fransen Winget, who founded the series. The lectureship was initiated in 1991 with Thomas Langford for the purpose of "bringing outstanding guest theologians to NTS." Presenters for this lectureship have included Theodore Runyon, Donald Bloesch, and Jürgen Moltmann.

The title of this monograph series indicates how we understand its character and purpose. First, even though the lectureships are geared toward biblical literature *and* systematic theology, we believe that the language of "theological explorations" is as appropriate to an engagement with Scripture as it is to an engagement with contemporary systematic theology. Though it is legitimate to approach at least some biblical texts with nontheological questions, we do not believe that doing so is to approach them *as Scripture*. Old and New Testament texts are not inert containers from which to draw theological insights; they are already witnesses to a serious theological engagement with particular historical, social, and political situations. Hence, biblical texts should be approached *on their own terms* through asking theological questions. Our intent, then, is that this series will be characterized by theological explorations from the fields of biblical studies and systematic theology.

Second, the word "explorations" is appropriate since we ask the lecturers to explore the cutting edge of their current interests and thinking. With the obvious time limitations of three public lectures, even their expanded versions will generally result not in long, detailed monographs but rather in shorter, suggestive treatments of a given topic—that is, explorations.

Finally, with the language of "the church catholic," we intend to convey our hope that these volumes should be *pro ecclesia* in the broadest sense—given by lecturers representing a variety of theological traditions for the benefit of the whole church of Jesus Christ. We at NTS have been generously gifted by those who fund these two lectureships. Our hope and prayer is that this series will become a generous gift to the church catholic, one means of equipping the people of God for participation in the *missio Dei*.

Andy Johnson
Lectures Coordinator
Nazarene Theological Seminary
Kansas City, Missouri

PREFACE

This book began life as the Earle Lectures at the Nazarene Theological Seminary in Kansas City, Missouri, on November 16–17, 2015. I had a great few days there, enjoying the company and conversation of faculty, staff, and students and being generously wined and dined. I would like to record my particular thanks to President Carla Sunberg for the hospitality of the institution, and to Andy Johnson for making the arrangements, chauffeuring me around town, and generally looking after me.

The expansion of the three shortish lectures into a book took place during the summer of 2016 in Durham, where I continue to savor having an office in Abbey House, which is one of the best offices one could ever hope for, with just about enough space for my books (though piles on the floor are slowly appearing) and with evergreen views of Palace Green and Durham Cathedral.

I received some valuable bibliographic help from my teaching assistant, Vasile Condrea. Douglas Earl has kindly done the indexing for me in a way that we hope is reader-friendly. I am grateful also to my patient and long-suffering friends who have again read something I have written in draft form and enabled me to make it better. Richard Briggs's questions about the structure and direction of the argument helped me see that I needed to be much clearer and more disciplined. Anthony Bash weeded out some irritating and/or infelicitous idioms. Chris Hays helped with bibliography. David Day gave an assist with the title (though the Baker Academic team also contributed). Both Patrick Morrow and my wife, Jenny, pointed out numerous small problems of wording and thought, enabling me to avoid factual errors and also to improve what I say. Tim West has been the copyeditor that every writer hopes for. Last but by no means least, Jim Kinney made wise editorial suggestions. I had been a little uncertain about structure and rhetoric in one or two places, especially in chapter 4, but it was only when Jim stated the obvious that I too saw that it was indeed the obvious, and was able to rewrite accordingly. As ever, such infelicities and errors as remain are all my own work.

ABBREVIATIONS

Aen.	Virgil, *Aeneid*
BHS	*Biblia Hebraica Stuttgartensia*. Edited by K. Elliger and W. Rudolph. Stuttgart: Deutsche Bibelgesellschaft, 1983.
BJS	Brown Judaic Studies
ca.	*circa*, about
CBSC	Cambridge Bible for Schools and Colleges
CCSL	Corpus Christianorum: Series Latina
ch(s).	chapter(s)
CSCD	Cambridge Studies in Christian Doctrine
esp.	especially
FC	Fathers of the Church
ITC	International Theological Commentary
JSOTSup	Journal for the Study of the Old Testament Supplement Series
NETS	*A New English Translation of the Septuagint*. Edited by Albert Pietersma and Benjamin G. Wright. New York and Oxford: Oxford University Press, 2007.

NRSV	New Revised Standard Version
OCT	Oxford Classical Texts
OSHT	Oxford Studies in Historical Theology
OTL	Old Testament Library
OTT	Old Testament Theology
WBC	Word Biblical Commentary

INTRODUCTION

In this book I offer a fresh (I hope) account of the nature of the Bible and of appropriate attitudes towards it and ways of reading it. I consider something of what is involved in regarding the Bible as a vehicle for faith in God today in a disenchanted world—that is, a world in which faith and God seem ever less comprehensible or meaningful to an increasing proportion of the population, whose deepest intuitions and hopes (at least insofar as they are consciously articulated) are oriented elsewhere. I also consider some aspects of what kind of scholarly study is best suited to do justice to the Bible, should one's interest in it be primarily that of regarding it as a vehicle for faith in God today.

On most reckonings, there is a close link between the content of the Bible and the content of Christian faith, at least in general terms—hence the importance of discussing approaches to the Bible in relation to questions about faith. Consider a summary account of biblical content such as: "God has made and sustains this world, and in it He calls a people, Israel and the church, to know and serve Him, to resist sin and evil, and to implement His priorities for life in its fullness. Through God's grace and through faith in Jesus Christ, we come to know God and to be part of His people, and thereby know ourselves to be beloved, accountable, and invited to eternal joy." Whatever the merits of this as a summary of biblical content—and any summary account will be debatable in terms of what is and is not included, and how it is put—it depicts a "big picture" whose acceptance or rejection is in certain ways equivalent to acceptance or rejection of Christian faith and identity. For the Bible offers a vision of the world in which right and wrong matter profoundly (far more than success and failure), alongside a divine grace that defies moral calculations. It offers a vision of the world in which, whatever the disappointments and sufferings and tragedies, there can be hope of an ultimate goodness and wonder beyond human imagining. However much discussions about the Bible tend to focus on more mundane and specific concerns (not least hot-button contemporary issues of gender and sexuality), the importance of the big picture needs to be kept in mind to appreciate what is really at stake.

I have no concern to try to offer apparently irresistible arguments for "believing the Bible." There are indeed good reasons for having faith in God and for trusting the Bible, and I will try to indicate some of them, but the skeptic who wants to remain skeptical will also not lack good arguments.[1] I am, however, interested in giving an account of the processes that are regularly at work if and when people do come to have faith and to trust what they read in the Bible. In other words, I am concerned not only with the *why* but also with the *how* in relation to faith and the Bible.

1. In the extensive literature on the nature of faith and why one might believe, two fine recent accounts are John Cottingham's *Why Believe?* (London and New York: Continuum, 2009) and his companion volume, *How to Believe* (London and New York: Bloomsbury, 2015). There is also a spicily robust and readable account in Francis Spufford's *Unapologetic: Why, Despite Everything, Christianity Can Still Make Surprising Emotional Sense* (London: Faber & Faber, 2012). Notable among the literature of autobiographical narratives is Andrew Klavan, *The Great Good Thing: A Secular Jew Comes to Faith in Christ* (Nashville: Nelson, 2016).

I am writing as a Christian (Anglican) and a professional scholar, in a way that I hope will make sense to a wide range of Christians of differing traditions and also be accessible and meaningful to those without faith. I do not suppose that all readers will like what I say. Some will no doubt critique my account of the Bible and faith as too thin. Others will no doubt critique me for claiming too much, and maybe even regard it as outrageous that an account of faith in God through the Bible should still be offered at all by a scholar who is employed by a secular British university in the twenty-first century. Nonetheless, in the hope of managing and directing readers' expectations, I would like at the outset to say a few words about what I am, and am not, trying to do.

Two Caveats

First, it is perilous to generalize about the Bible, either in terms of its content or in terms of attitudes towards it both within and outside the churches. Its content is so diverse in form and expression, and attitudes towards it are so variegated and complex, that any generalization will necessarily have to pass over numerous exceptions and qualifications that might be made. Nonetheless, I propose to put forward a particular thesis about the Bible as a whole, though I will discuss less than 1 percent of its content; and this approach will no doubt fail to address difficult issues that some readers might hope to find addressed here. I ask that allowance be made from the outset for the restrictions of my particular focus. I hope, however, that the approach will be justified by its practical fruitfulness in enabling at least some specific issues to be seen more clearly.

Second, throughout the book, unless I specify otherwise, I discuss the Christian Bible, comprising the Old and New Testaments. I do so with awareness of, and without prejudice towards, the distinct Jewish understanding of Bible as Tanakh: the Law, the Prophets, and the Writings. Although I hope that aspects of what I say might have some applicability in a Jewish frame of reference—and I shall sometimes refer to the importance of Jewish as well as Christian attitudes towards their Scriptures— the distinctive dynamics of a Jewish frame of reference require a different discussion.[2]

How Should the Credibility of the Bible Be Construed?

One of the main things I am hoping to do is to provide an understanding of the Bible and faith that will serve as an alternative to one particular account that is commonly encountered. I have in mind the long history in modernity of attacks on, and defenses of, the Bible and its credibility that have been couched in the categories of historical reliability or unreliability—though this is something that I can depict here only with the broadest of brushstrokes. I need at least briefly to clarify at the outset why my own account of faith and the Bible will not take this route.

It is undoubtedly the case that many people consider the Bible to be more trustworthy if it can be shown to be based on accurate historical facts. This is attested by a mass of literature, both scholarly and popular. The underlying logic often apparently revolves around some form of the question, how could the historically unreliable be the religiously reliable? Put positively: if the Bible can be shown to be accurate where it can be tested in matters of historical fact, then it becomes more reasonable to take it on faith—that is, to believe it—when it says things that are not amenable to historical verification. There is an obvious logic to this, which is presumably why it has wide appeal. That logic is related to the distinctive Christian contention that at a

2. Some of the key issues that I discuss are fascinatingly and extensively handled within a specifically Jewish frame of reference by Benjamin D. Sommer in *Revelation and Authority: Sinai in Jewish Scripture and Tradition* (New Haven and London: Yale University Press, 2015).

particular time and place, God became human in Jesus, who was crucified under Pontius Pilate. How can this particularity be maintained, if not by its historical veracity?

Nonetheless, there are at least two basic difficulties with such an approach. First, it is unclear why accurate historical evidence should produce faith in the living God. It is perfectly possible for someone to grant that there is much reliable historical material in the Bible and yet be disinclined to believe in the God of the Bible. Other factors must also come into play, and these other factors are likely to be decisive. Even in the case of the resurrection of Jesus, accepting that the tomb was empty and that Jesus was raised to life does not necessarily lead to Christian faith. One might suppose, for example, that Jesus, like Lazarus, died again in due course. A conviction that Jesus was raised would lead to Christian faith only if one also accepts the particular construal of the resurrection that Paul presents, that "Christ, being raised from the dead, will never die again; death no longer has dominion over him" (Rom. 6:9), and that this creates a new reality into which others too can enter. Of course, it can still be argued that historical reliability plays a necessary critical role—if the event did not happen, its supposed meaning is empty—but this leads into the second difficulty.

The modern categories of "history" and "historical reliability" are more problematic to apply to the biblical text than is often realized. Although the writers of the great Old Testament narratives and of the Gospels were undoubtedly concerned with things that happened in the past, their approach to their material is not that of modern historiography or the modern analytical historian. In many ways it is closer to the approach of the historical novelist or dramatist, with a concern to speak to the present through creative use of the past (perhaps often akin to the notion of "cultural memory"). We can create an insoluble problem if we appraise the Bible in relation to our

own preferred categories without sufficiently trying to discover
what its own preferred categories and conventions are.

There is a sense in which the biblical writers anticipated some of the conventions of the modern movie. For example, when the pharaoh's daughter
adopted Moses, "she named him Moses [Hebrew *mōsheh*], 'because,' she
said, 'I drew him out [*māshāh*] of the water'" (Exod. 2:10). Modern scholars
have often pointed to a note of historical authenticity here, in that the name
Moses looks to be a genuinely Egyptian name, akin to Tut*mose* or Ra*meses*.
Well and good. However, the story straightforwardly attributes the name to
the pharaoh's daughter, an Egyptian, making a pun in Hebrew, the language
of Israel. Although some ancient rabbis ingeniously suggested that perhaps
she was so sympathetic to the Hebrew people that she took lessons in learning their language, such rationalizing is extraneous to the story's own frame
of reference and misreads its genre and literary conventions. Rather, the
narrator is using the common dramatic convention whereby all characters
operate in the language of the target audience.

In addition, the narrator, like a movie camera, enables the reader/viewer
to be where they need to be, when they need to be there. So, for example,
when David and Goliath speak on the battlefield, we know exactly what they
say (1 Sam. 17:43–47). We are not positioned somewhere in the ranks of
the Israelite army, struggling to hear what is being said somewhere ahead of
us; we are up close, seeing and hearing. And we are similarly up close for a
conversation between Israel's king and his chief of staff, as Saul speaks with
Abner about David at the very time that David is going out on the battlefield
(17:55–56). We, like the narrator, are free of mundane constraints, so that
we are privy to the story, just as in movies.

In Luke's account of Jesus in Gethsemane, Jesus prays in such anguish
that "his sweat [becomes] like great drops of blood falling down on the
ground" (Luke 22:44).[3] Here Luke's narration serves as the equivalent of a
zoom lens. It is the middle of the night (admittedly, with a full moon around
Passover), and Jesus' disciples are a short distance away, struggling unsuc-
cessfully to stay awake. Yet we, the readers, are brought right up close, just
a few feet away, so that we can see great drops of sweat on Jesus' face and
understand something of the depth of his anguished prayer. The narrator,
like the camera, is free from mundane constraints and thus enables us to be
where we could not be otherwise; no eyewitness was actually close enough

---

3. There are interesting text-critical questions about the status of this verse, but
they do not really affect the point at issue, as the literary conventions that we see
here are present elsewhere in Luke's Gospel.

to see sweat on Jesus. To recognize the conventions with which the narrator works—conventions sometimes summarily described by the literary category "omniscient narrator"—makes the text resistant to certain kinds of historical analysis. This is not because Jesus did not pray in Gethsemane, but because the narrative portrayal is cast in a dramatic and engaging mode.

My argument in this book is an alternative to an "evidentialist" approach to belief in relation to God and to the Bible. I do not at all wish to deny that there is substantive historical content in the Bible, or that Jesus was raised from the dead, or that questions of historical reliability can often play a significant role in people coming to, or maintaining, or losing, faith. Not least, this is because people are accustomed to issues of faith and the Bible being framed in this way. My thesis, however, is that to start here, and to frame issues accordingly, is not the best place to start, and indeed that it risks skewing important issues. I propose that it would be good for the high road of arguments over historical reliability to become a road rather less traveled. In its place I will propose the desirability of taking a journey of biblical exploration in the company of people both past and present whom one has good reason to trust.

Two Notes to the Reader

One convention I use is to put certain paragraphs or sections in smaller type, as already seen above. There are also three excursuses (at the end of chs. 1, 2, and 4), which are essentially smaller-type sections that have been removed from the main argument lest they make it unduly cluttered. The main argument of the book can be read without these smaller-type sections and excursuses. For those who are interested, however, these amplify and clarify some facet of the argument and/or deal with a possible difficulty. They also contain occasional asides.

Another convention I use is to capitalize pronouns and possessive adjectives when they refer to God—for example, "He," "His." There is an in-principle issue of classic theology that God is beyond gender as we understand it. Moreover, in light of this, feminists have objected to continued use of masculine terms for God (Does it privilege male over female? Does it deify the male?). Nonetheless, I think that there are still good reasons for retaining traditional gendered language in capitalized form. First, it is a long-standing reverential tradition on the part of both Jews and Christians that is worth reclaiming in the not-very-reverentially-inclined culture of today. Second, this usage stands in continuity with the Bible's own gendered usage, yet seeks through capitalization to indicate that such language, when predicated of God, has a significance other than that in human predication. In other words, my capitalization is intended to be a modest pointer towards the affirmation of God as beyond gender as we understand it.

Posing the Problem

Introduction

I hope I may be permitted, as an Englishman, to begin with some words from the coronation service of the present queen, Elizabeth II, in Westminster Abbey on June 2, 1953. At an early point in the ceremony the archbishop of Canterbury, together with the moderator of the General Assembly of the Church of Scotland, presented a copy of the Bible to the queen. The archbishop said:

> Our gracious Queen:
> to keep your Majesty ever mindful of the law and the
> Gospel of God
> as the Rule for the whole life and government of Chris-
> tian Princes,
> we present you with this Book,
> the most valuable thing that this world affords.

The moderator then said:

> Here is Wisdom;
> This is the Royal Law;
> These are the lively Oracles of God.[1]

In these few but weighty words, the Bible is understood to be an artifact of this world that contains the living word of God and so is of incomparable value. It is symbolically presented to the queen at the outset of her reign because its content is understood to be fundamental to her vocation to public life with great responsibilities for other people.

Such an understanding, like any other understanding in the world, is of course contestable. The Bible and its presence in the coronation service would now be regarded by many as, at best, quaint, and mainly as a testimony to the remarkably persistent influence of the religious and political ideologies of the seventeenth century (and earlier), rather than as a good guide to what matters in the modern world. Moreover, I imagine that when the queen's successor is crowned, there will be battles royal over the wording of this and other parts of the ceremony. Whether the presentation of the Christian Bible, with the words "the most valuable thing that this world affords," will survive to be used in the next coronation is, I suspect, a moot point.

Nonetheless, in these words we have a way into the subject matter of this book. For the wording of the coronation service on one level simply expresses, no doubt in a rather Protestant formulation, a classic Christian understanding of the significance of the Bible: that it is the word of God in human words, which can give incomparably valuable wisdom and guidance for life in this world.

1. See http://www.oremus.org/liturgy/coronation/cor1953b.html.

I appreciate that "the word of God in human words" privileges the genre of Old Testament prophecy, whose self-presentation takes this form, and only relates more obliquely to other literary genres such as narrative, psalm, proverb, gospel, letter, or apocalypse. Nonetheless, there is good Christian precedent for using this or similar wording as shorthand for the Bible as a whole, and for convenience I retain it here.

Of course, this Christian understanding has rarely been uncontroversial; rather, it has been a perennial subject of debate. In the first few centuries of the church, Christian thinkers had to defend their faith from attack by others, and the role of the Bible tended to be central in such debates, of which a paradigm is perhaps Origen's *Against Celsus* in the third century. Within Christian cultures there has been constant discussion, in one way or another, about how best to understand what is, and is not, entailed by believing that the Bible gives God's truth in human language. But ever since the privileged position of Christian churches in Western society began to be questioned and eroded in modern times, from the seventeenth century onwards, the belief that the Bible gives divine truth in human words has been increasingly questioned and doubted, and often simply ridiculed and rejected. Some form of an Enlightenment critique of the Bible is probably a default position for most people in the UK and Europe, and also for many in other parts of the world today.

Those who, like me, wish to uphold and commend the classic Christian understanding of the Bible have a large task on their hands on any reckoning. Nonetheless, there are various factors that I hope make a fresh expression of this issue timely. On the one hand, the diminished and still further diminishing role of the churches in once-Christian but now increasingly secularized societies, especially in Europe and North America,[2]

2. There are many questions about the nature of secularization, not least in relation to a certain resurgence of religion in the public arena in recent years. But the diminution of historic forms of Christian faith is hardly in doubt.

means that churches in these regions need to do some learning: learning no longer to take for granted understandings and assumptions that seemed natural in the past; learning how to conduct themselves as a minority; and learning to present their distinctive understanding of life, faith, and truth accordingly.

On the other hand, both the social and the intellectual worlds in which Enlightenment critiques of the Bible and the churches were formulated have also disappeared, and the developments of thought and life of recent years, often summed up (for better or worse) as "postmodern," offer a fresh context and new challenges for articulating a Christian understanding of things. I hope that the discussion that follows will lead us to engage at least some of these intellectual and existential challenges.

> I apologize for the limitations of the mainly Eurocentric perspective of my presentation, when I am well aware that many of the most dynamic contexts of contemporary Christian faith, and not least of my own Anglican Communion, are located in the Southern Hemisphere and beyond the historic areas of Christian culture.[3] Churches in China, for example, have always needed to handle themselves as a minority. The fact that Eurocentric debates and perspectives in relation to the Bible have been influential worldwide means, I hope, that much of what I say will resonate widely. I recognize, however, that in terms of contemporary Christian attitudes and challenges worldwide, my approach may sometimes feel a little parochial. Nonetheless—to misquote Luther—I stand here, and I cannot do otherwise.

Setting the Scene

Benjamin Jowett and "Interpreting the Scripture like Any Other Book"

I would like briefly to consider another moment in English history. In March 1860 there appeared one of the most controversial works of Christian theology ever published in England:

3. An excellent introductory account is Philip Jenkins's *The Next Christendom: The Coming of Global Christianity*, 3rd ed. (Oxford: Oxford University Press, 2011).

Essays and Reviews.[4] When I read the book today I find its contributions mostly thoughtful and worthwhile, though also a bit dull; so it is hard to appreciate how notorious and controversial the book was when it was first published. But *Essays and Reviews* appeared at a time when the social and intellectual world was changing quickly. It is perhaps indicative that the other famous book published around this time in England (five months previously, in November 1859) was Charles Darwin's *On the Origin of Species*.

Probably the single most controversial essay in *Essays and Reviews* was "On the Interpretation of Scripture" by the Oxford classical scholar Benjamin Jowett.[5] In this essay Jowett was concerned with how Christian faith appeared to him to be losing touch with educated thought. He reckoned that this tended to take one or both of two forms. Either the study of the Bible was defensive and blinkered, in a reactionary posture towards the new insights and learning of the modern world, and/or the study was fanciful and undisciplined, in a way that made biblical meaning appear more or less arbitrary. In Jowett's judgment, each tendency obscured the Bible's real character and true value. Each also contributed to a wider problem represented by the church's use of the Bible—that is, each allowed understandings and issues that had arisen over the ages to get in the way of reading and understanding the Bible in itself in a disciplined and attentive way. To remedy these faults, Jowett put forward one basic precept for biblical interpretation: *"Interpret the Scripture like any other book."*[6] He did not see this precept as undermining the dignity and significance of the Bible. Rather,

4. There is a convenient (and compendious) presentation of the text of *Essays and Reviews* with notes and commentary in *Essays and Reviews: The 1860 Text and Its Reading*, ed. Victor Shea and William Whitla (Charlottesville and London: University Press of Virginia, 2000).

5. Jowett, "On the Interpretation of Scripture," in Shea and Whitla, *Essays and Reviews*, 477–536.

6. Jowett, "On the Interpretation of Scripture," 504. Italics original.

the opposite was true: "When interpreted like any other book, by the same rules of evidence and the same canons of criticism, the Bible will still remain unlike any other book." The results of banishing the defensive and the fanciful would be entirely beneficial: "[The Bible's] beauty will be freshly seen, as of a picture which is restored after many ages to its original state."[7]

In saying this, Jowett envisaged something rather straightforward and commonsensical (and he had already developed the basic idea in a pamphlet in 1848, though this had attracted no notice).[8] Moreover, strikingly, he made no appeal whatsoever to the new and controversial mode of biblical scholarship, the "higher criticism," then being developed in Germany.

> The way in which many nineteenth-century British historical and biblical scholars were significantly unaware of their German counterparts, failing to appreciate how some of the basic interpretive frames of reference were changing, is memorably captured in George Eliot's depiction of Casaubon, as interpreted by Ladislaw to Dorothea, in *Middlemarch* (1871). Erudition is not enough, for the quality of the conceptual frame of reference within which factual knowledge is deployed makes all the difference.

Jowett thought the issue was simple: just read the Bible as one reads other classical texts, such as those of Plato or Sophocles, on which Jowett worked in his capacity as Regius Professor of Greek. He asked, "Who would write a bulky treatise about the method to be pursued in interpreting Plato or Sophocles?"[9] The language and thought of these ancient authors can sometimes be challenging, but good philological learning nonetheless makes their works accessible, and the content of these ancient classics can readily be appreciated as rich and enduring, whatever their possible time-bound limitations, which must also

7. Jowett, "On the Interpretation of Scripture," 503.

8. Peter Hinchliff, *Benjamin Jowett and the Christian Religion* (Oxford: Clarendon, 1987), 31–32.

9. Jowett, "On the Interpretation of Scripture," 504.

be acknowledged. Just as the restoration of a great picture, through having accumulated dirt and touch-ups by perhaps inferior hands removed, enables someone today to appreciate the power of the original in a fresh way, Jowett supposed that if a modern reader is enabled to read the biblical documents in their intrinsic original meaning, without the dulling overlay of centuries of often fanciful or misguided commentary, the result should surely only be gain. Behind the complexities of Christian doctrinal systems and misguided readings, one can recover the original simplicity of Christian truth.

> This approach is expounded at length by Jowett's friend, F. W. Farrar, in his 1885 Bampton Lectures, *History of Interpretation*,[10] which are dedicated to Jowett. Farrar gives a rather scathing account of classic biblical interpretation as, in essence, a history of misinterpretation from which contemporary readers need to be rescued. Erroneous systems of interpretation arose for many reasons, primary among which was philological ignorance: "The original Hebrew of the Old Testament was for many ages unknown to the Christian Church, and when Greek also became an unknown language to all except a few, the caprice of interpreters was freed from all important checks. . . . All Exegesis must be unsound which is not based on the literal, grammatical, historical contextual sense of the sacred writers" (xi, xxv). The responsible modern reader has to set aside the more or less misguided interpretive systems of the past: "He who would study Scripture in its integrity and purity must approach the sacred page 'with a mind washed clean from human opinions'" (xxv). Farrar, like Jowett, offers his work in the service of retrieving the "simplicity" and "universality" of the biblical text (xi).

Yet Jowett's essay met with a generally hostile reception, which surprised and shocked him. As one commentator puts it, Jowett "offended just about everyone who was not a Broad Churchman or unbeliever."[11] No less a person than the future British prime minister, Mr. Gladstone, penciled negative comments throughout

10. London: Macmillan, 1886.
11. James R. Moore, ed., *Religion in Victorian Britain*, vol. 3, *Sources* (Manchester, UK: Manchester University Press, 1988), 26.

the margins of his copy of Jowett's essay, and finally commented on the whole: "A cold, vain, barren Philosophy, ending with the Grave here. The sport and Triumph of devils hereafter."[12]

Overall, the outcry does not reflect well upon the general levels of biblical and theological literacy in Victorian England. What particularly strikes me is the level of mutual incomprehension. Jowett was writing as a scholarly and well-intentioned Christian believer who saw genuine problems in the way that many of his contemporaries were handling Scripture. Many of those who clamored against Jowett and considered him a heretic clearly had little grasp either of what Jowett was really proposing or of why he was proposing it, and made too little attempt to arrive at any genuine understanding of his position. But despite the sheer ignorance and prejudice on the part of so many of those who opposed Jowett, I think that they nonetheless may not have been mistaken in sensing that something important was at risk, even if they were incapable of articulating well what that was. Similarly, Jowett himself had little awareness of possible deep difficulties with his argument or of why responsible Christians might legitimately take exception to it. In other words, I suggest that not only Jowett but also his opponents had important intuitions about the Bible and its interpretation; but they also had major blind spots, such that more heat than light was generated by the debates at the time.

Unfortunately, it is not possible here to do a proper study of the history of ideas.[13] Rather, my appeal to Jowett is essentially symbolic. I want to take his proposal for "interpreting

---

12. Hinchliff, *Benjamin Jowett*, 96.

13. An illuminating account of what Jowett was and was not trying to do in his famous essay is provided by James Barr, "Jowett and the Reading of the Bible 'Like Any Other Book,'" in *Bible and Interpretation: The Collected Essays of James Barr*, vol. 1, *Interpretation and Theology*, ed. John Barton (Oxford: Oxford University Press, 2013), 169–97. Among other things, Barr shows how idiosyncratic Jowett was, and how he stood well apart from what became the mainstream of modern historical-critical scholarship.

the Scripture like any other book" as a notion in its own right, which, irrespective of Jowett's own particular concerns, over time became symbolic of a mainstream approach in modern Western culture. That is, the Bible's status as Scripture—which is a shorthand term for a cluster of religious attitudes and theological understandings related to the Bible, including the fact that certain documents should be recognized as constituting the Bible in the first place—should be set aside and make no difference to the way in which its content is interpreted. Rather, biblical documents should be interpreted in the same way as other ancient documents, an approach that over time has come to be known, also in shorthand, as "the historical-critical approach." This approach has been generally, though not universally, welcomed by Christian scholars for reasons similar to those of Jowett: it enables an honest approach to the material that can dispense with special pleading and allow the material's intrinsic meaning and qualities to become more clearly apparent.

A nice example of the way in which Christian scholars can still feel the need to make the kind of argument that Jowett made, and to do so apparently for similar reasons (i.e., defensive and out-of-touch attitudes to the Bible within the churches), is a fairly recent (1999) essay by the Roman Catholic biblical scholar Benedict Viviano, "The Historical-Critical Method in Modern Biblical Studies: Yes or No?"[14] Viviano writes to counter doubts on the part of some as to the value of historical-critical work, and so argues that the appropriate answer to the question posed in his title should—"in an academic context and to some extent in the church"—be "an emphatic *yes.*"[15] His interesting argument is essentially twofold.

On the one hand, he argues that cultural reasons—the "historical turn" in Western civilization since the eighteenth century—necessitated

14. Viviano, "The Historical-Critical Method in Modern Biblical Studies: Yes or No?," in *Catholic Hermeneutics Today: Critical Essays* (Eugene, OR: Cascade, 2014), 1–13.
15. Viviano, "Historical-Critical Method," 1, 13.

the adoption of historical-critical work with regard to the Bible. This required, among other things, reading biblical documents like other ancient documents:

> A historical, critically historical method had become indispensable, an absolute necessity, if the Bible were to be rescued from the rationalists, its educated despisers, even if this meant offending the *devots*.
>
> Concretely, this meant that, at least initially, as a first step, the historical parts of the Bible had to be read as one read Herodotus and Thucydides; the prophets and psalmists read as one read other ancient poets, Hesiod and Sophocles; the biblical laws as comparable to those of Solon and the early Romans; biblical wisdom as one read the Stoics and Epicureans. Historical analogy must prevail. Comparisons must be made with the world outside the Bible. Only then could the Bible begin to be understood in its original context. Only then could its proper contribution be appreciated, its religious and salvific value be seen in its full splendor, its dangers avoided. Only then could the mockers be silenced, indeed, intrigued and, God willing, converted to a better mind. The real risks involved were outweighed by the hoped-for advantages.[16]

On the other hand, Viviano seeks to root this approach within the Bible itself. Insofar as the best analogy to making historical judgments about the past is judicial processes, in which evidence and witnesses are analyzed and evaluated in a fair way, then the biblical injunctions to the exercise of impartial judgment on the part of those handling legal cases (Lev. 19:15; Deut. 1:17) should be applicable by analogy to the evaluation of evidence and witnesses within the Bible. Moreover, the Bible's own characteristic practice is to present multiple versions of the same events: two accounts of creation, two versions of the Decalogue, and four different Gospels "which cry out for comparative analysis." Thus it can be seen that the questions characteristic of historical-critical work "are not foreign to the Bible but are present within the Bible itself and some of the principles for their resolution are also present in the Bible."[17]

Overall, Viviano is upbeat about the enormous gains to be derived from historical-critical work, and he notes that its acknowledgment in the Second Vatican Council led to theological and pastoral renewal in the church.[18] I cite Viviano to show that a contemporary scholar can still make an argument

---

16. Viviano, "Historical-Critical Method," 3–4.
17. Viviano, "Historical-Critical Method," 3–4, 9, 10.
18. Viviano, "Historical-Critical Method," 5.

analogous to that of Jowett, both in what he says and, as will be seen, in what he does not say. Jowett's precedent remains a live option.

One terminological note. The "historical-critical approach" is not infrequently called the "historical-critical method," as by Viviano. This, however, is potentially misleading. What is at stake is an overall stance towards the material and its interpretation: that the biblical documents should be interpreted in the way that other ancient documents are interpreted. Such a stance, or approach, uses any and every appropriate scholarly method to try to get at a better understanding of the material in question—whether that be source criticism, redaction criticism, psychological criticism, gender criticism, or any other critical method that is found productive. The issue is *an approach* that utilizes *many methods*.

One major difficulty, however, that has generally been too little addressed, is that most Christian scholars who advocate approaching the biblical documents "like any other book" nonetheless still take for granted the (in one way or another) *privileged* status of the biblical documents and see no need to make a case for this privilege. That is, they assume that certain documents constitute a Bible, that biblical content merits extensive and searching historical and comparative study, and that the results of such study will highlight the special qualities of the material and its enduring significance for knowing God. In other words, the book itself remains in some way unlike other books. But unless some account is offered as to *why* the Bible is *not* like any other book, it becomes ever less clear that one should continue to value and privilege the Bible and its content in the first place. Why bother to study these ancient documents rather than others, and why assume that the results of one's study should have more than antiquarian or general cultural interest today?

Benedict Viviano, for example (in the above small-type section), takes for granted the privileged status of the biblical documents, and sees no need to discuss or justify this assumption. The result of proper historical study is that the Bible's "religious and salvific value [is] seen in its full splendor"—to which Jowett would presumably say "Amen." But why make that Christian assumption? What if one does not grant that the Bible has "salvific value"? Why read Hesiod and Sophocles in order better to understand the biblical prophets and psalmists, rather than reading them all as variants of particular kinds of ancient literature in which Hesiod and Sophocles may have as much value and splendor as the biblical poets, or even more? All alike may be fine literature; none need be seen as salvific.

My concern is not to question the value of historical-critical work, even though it is a more complex phenomenon than is sometimes appreciated.[19] Nor is it to deny that the Bible can be legitimately read and studied for nonreligious reasons, as will be discussed in the next chapter. Rather, it is to observe that Christian scholars such as Jowett and Viviano confidently argue for the value of reading the Bible "like any other book" in the way that they do because the in-some-way-privileged status of the Bible in itself is taken for granted and so can be left out of the argument. That privileging of the Bible is part of the very nature of Christian identity and understanding. In the past, when Western cultures also acknowledged a Christian identity, little or no defense of that privileging was necessary because it was not called for. Today, however, in an increasingly post-Christian culture, the privileged status of the Bible is itself a contentious issue and needs to be justified if it is to be maintained. This does not mean that the positive concerns represented by interpreting the Bible "like any other book" need to be set aside. But it does mean that they need to be complemented by other concerns and arguments of a different nature—and so may also need some reformulation and/or reframing in the process.

19. The nature and purpose of historical-critical work when it was first articulated and adopted, and some of the intrinsic ambiguities in such work, are compellingly set out by Michael Legaspi in *The Death of Scripture and the Rise of Biblical Studies*, OSHT (Oxford: Oxford University Press, 2010).

The Modern Diminution of the Bible's Scope and Reliability

If Jowett usefully articulates what came to be shorthand for a distinctively modern approach to the study of the Bible, it will also be helpful at least briefly to note some of the wider cultural and intellectual developments, many already prior to Jowett, that made such a program seem widely attractive.

What role should the Bible have in one's life? The classic Christian position is that the Bible should shape one's understanding of the world as a whole, as a corollary of having faith in God through Jesus. Here we have "the lively oracles of God," the one true God whose will and purposes for creation are made accessible: through this book, believers should come to understand the world, themselves, and their role and responsibilities within the world. Here is true guidance for both thought and life.

If one looks at the history of Western thought from the sixteenth to the nineteenth century, one can see the progressive collapse of this view, at least in the way it was then held. Generally speaking, understandings of the world in terms of both space and time increasingly diverged from what seemed to be presupposed and/or articulated within the Bible.

The period of the Renaissance and of the early modern world was one in which discoveries were made that enlarged people's understanding of the world's extent and its history. There were the voyages of discovery, perhaps especially the discovery of the Americas, which revealed a compass to the world that was unknown to the biblical writers, whose geography was much more narrowly conceived. The account of the peoples of the world in Genesis 10, for example, is tellingly restricted in this regard; in modern terms, it is the world of the Middle East. The New Testament world is somewhat larger—for example, the account of the nationalities of all the pilgrims in Jerusalem on the day of Pentecost (Acts 2:8–11) goes as far west as Rome—but is not really other than a major part of the Roman Empire: the Mediterranean world. As a consequence of the discoveries of new lands, histories of the world increasingly struggled to maintain the biblical frame of reference that had been regarded as one of the many corollaries of allowing the Bible to shape an understanding of the world.

One interesting example of the sense of increasing difficulty in maintaining world history within a biblical frame of reference is the seventeenth-century attempt by Isaac la Peyrère (1596–1676) to argue that the early chapters of Genesis tell only the history of the Jews, not of humanity as a whole.[20] His proposal, in his *Prae-Adamitae* (1655), is that there were humans before Adam, "pre-Adamites." This was an attempt to reconcile the biblical story with the evidence of wider cultures of great antiquity that were unknown to the biblical writers. Although the proposal clearly goes against the sense of the biblical text, it was a well-intentioned and intelligent attempt to resolve a difficult problem by bringing together the Bible with new knowledge. La Peyrère became notorious and generated much discussion (and rebuttal) at the time, but in due course his work fell by the wayside and was forgotten because its basic working assumption about some continuing role for the Bible in framing the history of humanity and the world ceased to have general intellectual purchase.

If space and time on earth were seen to be greater than in the biblical depiction, the same also applied to space and time beyond the earth. The famous early modern astronomical debates, for which the names of Copernicus and Galileo may serve as shorthand, eventually showed that the earth was not

---

20. A useful introduction is Heikki Räisänen's "The Bible and the Traditions of the Nations: Isaac la Peyrère as a Precursor of Biblical Criticism," in *Marcion, Muhammad and the Mahatma* (London: SCM, 1997), 137–52.

at the center of the universe (and even though the Bible never makes this claim, a central issue was how a Christian culture interpreted the Bible and understood the world). Rather, the earth is a modest-sized planet in orbit around a sun in a small galaxy, in a staggeringly immense universe ordered by the laws of physics (as formulated in due course by Isaac Newton and others).

In general cultural terms, the natural sciences became increasingly definitive for understanding the world and life within it. The complex and multifaceted history towards which I am gesturing is, on one level, uncontroversial. As the European mind acquired new knowledge about the workings of the world and was also steadily secularized, the status and role of the Bible were correspondingly transformed and diminished. The history of ideas is, however, much less straightforward than many a culturally dominant narrative of "the triumph of science over religion" would have it, and this is increasingly recognized in recent literature.[21]

In the wider culture, the Bible over time went from being the lens for seeing the world (and oneself) to being only an interesting object within it. The Bible became a collection of ancient writings with intrinsic historical interest as a window (or windows) onto the ancient world, and also a cultural artifact and influence within Western civilization; but it was no longer a focal point for existential trust in God and a guide to life and thought in the here and now.

21. A readable and entertaining introduction is *Galileo Goes to Jail, and Other Myths about Science and Religion*, ed. Ronald L. Numbers (Cambridge, MA: Harvard University Press, 2009). Peter Harrison's various books unfailingly shed fresh light on this history of ideas; see, e.g., *The Territories of Science and Religion* (Chicago and London: University of Chicago Press, 2015). A fundamental reappraisal of what is at stake theologically in this history is provided by Nicholas Lash's *The Beginning and the End of 'Religion'* (Cambridge: Cambridge University Press, 1995). Among other things, Lash develops the implications of Michael Buckley's groundbreaking *At the Origins of Modern Atheism* (New Haven and London: Yale University Press, 1987).

The Marginalizing of God and the "Humanizing" of the Bible

One important corollary to this diminishing of the scope and significance of the Bible is a specifically theological issue. Put simply, it is the question, where is God?

On a classic Christian understanding, God is revealed in and through the Bible, and one learns from the Bible how to recognize God elsewhere. Although this revelation happens throughout the Bible, it is supremely focused on Jesus and on his portrayal in the New Testament. It was always recognized that the biblical documents had human authors, but these authors had generally been considered to be in an important sense open, or receptive, or in some way transparent to God; in the classic theological formulation, their writings were inspired by God (2 Tim. 3:16–17). This meant that God could be encountered in and through their human words. The human words were also in some sense the word of God.

However, modern scholarly work has characteristically focused on these human dimensions of the Bible in ways that have gone beyond precedents in the premodern period. More and more, scholars have concentrated on understanding the human language of the biblical writers as an end in itself: What does this language mean, as expressive of the outlooks of its writers, and what does it reveal about the world they lived in? Although such questions were not new, they tended now to be oriented in such a way that the question of how the Bible reveals and mediates God increasingly receded into the margins or the background. It became less a matter of "What did God say, or what does God say, through Jeremiah or Paul?" and more a matter of "What did Jeremiah or Paul think about God, and what does this reveal about the situations they were involved in?"

This approach was lucidly articulated in a programmatic way by one of the most influential of early modern thinkers,

Baruch (Benedict) Spinoza (1632–77). In the formative period of the seventeenth century, when discussing how to interpret the Bible, Spinoza wrote, "Great caution is necessary not to confound the mind of a prophet or historian with the mind of the Holy Spirit and the truth of the matter." This assertion was prefaced with the observation that scholars "are at work not on the truth of passages, but solely on their meaning" and that it is important "not to confound the meaning of a passage with its truth." Rather, the focus of biblical study should be "the life, the conduct, and the studies of the author of each book, who he was, what was the occasion, and the epoch of his writing, whom did he write for, and in what language. Further, it should inquire into the fate of each book, how it was first received . . ."[22] In such statements, the human and the divine are sharply distinguished, as are questions of meaning and truth, both of which distinctions in themselves are entirely valid. But whereas traditionally it had been believed that the biblical writers mediated God's purposes and promises—a mediation difficult to articulate precisely, but typically depicted with the language of "inspiration"—Spinoza set a new trend in biblical interpretation by leaving the relationship between the human and the divine, and between meaning and truth (other than in terms of matters of ancient history), undiscussed. Such questions are thereby moved to the margins, and arguably they are not needed at all.

The new mode of studying the theological content of the Bible became a history of religious thought/ideas. To be sure, this thought and these ideas were still generally assumed by Christians to have been in some way given by God, and God was not usually denied by biblical scholars, who at least until recently have been predominantly believers and, often, ordained

22. Various editions of Spinoza's *Tractatus/Treatise* are available. My edition is *Benedict de Spinoza: "A Theologico-Political Treatise" and "A Political Treatise,"* ed. and trans. R. H. M. Elwes (New York: Dover, 1951), 106, 103.

ministers. But the question of God in relation to the human dimensions of the biblical text received ever less attention and was apparently not considered necessary. Jowett, for example, did not discuss it anywhere in his lengthy essay. Meanwhile, in the wider culture, the reality of God increasingly was denied, for many and varied reasons, as the conditions and assumptions of modern life became over time increasingly less receptive to classic Christian faith and thought. As Richard Rorty puts it, "Getting rid of theology as part of the intellectual life of the West was not the achievement of one book, nor one man, nor one generation, nor one century."[23] It took a long time; but the results go wide and deep.

Charles Taylor, in *A Secular Age*,[24] offers a suggestive and probing account of the development of secularization in Western culture. Taylor gives prominence to the notion of disenchantment, by which he means a shift in the understanding of where meaning is to be found. Previously, meaning was considered to be inherent in the world, and so reality, in an important sense, made claims upon people to respond rightly. The classic biblical expressions of this are the portrayals of Wisdom in Proverbs 8 and the Word/Jesus in John 1 as realities immanent within creation, such that in gaining wisdom, or in coming to faith in Jesus, one enters more fully into reality as it truly is. But in a new, disenchanted understanding of the world, the sole source of meaning is the human mind. People no longer discern meaning in the world, but rather impose meaning on things that are external to their true, inner selves.

Consistent with such an overall move towards disenchantment, biblical interpretation shifted over time from being a

23. Richard Rorty, *Consequences of Pragmatism* (Minneapolis: University of Minnesota Press, 1982), 34.
24. Cambridge, MA: Belknap Press of Harvard University Press, 2005. An excellent guide to Taylor's thought in *A Secular Age* is James K. A. Smith, *How (Not) to Be Secular: Reading Charles Taylor* (Grand Rapids: Eerdmans, 2014).

matter of discerning the reality of God and the world and oneself in and through the biblical text (itself located in the context of the life and practices of Christian faith) to being a matter of seeing language about God as a human construction, which can certainly be used to understand the world insofar as it is found helpful, but which has no intrinsic relation to reality. While Christian faith remained culturally dominant, the sharp edge of this new approach could be blunted for many through assimilation into the existing frame of reference. But when Christian faith diminishes, and people ask in a new way why the Bible should be considered a better account of reality than any other resource, it is no longer clear what, if any, are the grounds for privileging the Bible.

Put differently: there is surely a significant analogy between the role one accords to the Bible and the role one accords to the Bible's God. My symbolic modern Christian scholar, Jowett, who argued for interpreting the Bible like any other book, still retained a belief, albeit unarticulated, that the Bible was in some way unlike any other book. Moreover, one finds in Jowett no argument that the God of the Bible should be understood "like any other god"; and such an argument he would no doubt have considered misguided and improper. Yet why interpret the Bible "like any other book" and not understand the God of the Bible to be "like any other god"? Other documents from the ancient Mediterranean and Near Eastern worlds depict many deities, and there are numerous similarities and continuities between these depictions and the biblical depictions. Why believe that the Bible portrays the one true God, while other ancient documents portray false gods / human constructs?

Unsurprisingly, this basic point is made with characteristic verve by Richard Dawkins:

I have found it an amusing strategy, when asked whether I am an atheist, to point out that the questioner is also an atheist when considering Zeus, Apollo, Amon Ra, Mithras, Baal, Thor, Wotan, the Golden Calf and the Flying Spaghetti Monster. I just go one god further.

All of us feel entitled to express extreme scepticism to the point of outright disbelief—except that in the case of unicorns, tooth fairies and the gods of Greece, Rome, Egypt and the Vikings, there is (nowadays) no need to bother. In the case of the Abrahamic God, however, there is a need to bother, because a substantial proportion of the people with whom we share this planet do believe strongly in his existence.[25]

There is a certain irony in this, which Dawkins may not fully appreciate, inasmuch as it was Jewish and Christian understandings of the one God that historically had great influence in leading people to dismiss beliefs in other gods. Nonetheless, Dawkins's point has real force in a contemporary context.

There is, of course, significant precedent for Dawkins's contention. One of his intellectual predecessors (though less militant and more ironic) in the first half of the twentieth century was H. L. Mencken, who composed a famous 1922 "Memorial Service" for the gods:

Where is the grave-yard of dead gods? What lingering mourner waters their mounds? There was a day when Jupiter was the king of the gods, and any man who doubted his puissance was *ipso facto* a barbarian and an ignoramus. But where in all the world is there a man who worships Jupiter today? And what of Huitzilpochtli? In one year—and it is no more than five hundred years ago—fifty thousand youths and maidens were slain in sacrifice to him. . . . But today Huitzilpochtli is as magnificently forgotten as Allen G. Thurman. . . . [Mencken then provides a long list of names of deities attested in "any good treatise on comparative religion" and concludes:] They were gods . . . of civilized peoples—worshiped and believed in by millions. All were theoretically omnipotent, omniscient and immortal. And all are dead.[26]

25. Richard Dawkins, *The God Delusion* (London: Bantam, 2006), 53–54.
26. Mencken, "Memorial Service," in *H. L. Mencken on Religion*, ed. S. T. Joshi (Amherst, NY: Prometheus, 2002), 293, 296–97.

In the terms of my discussion: If the Bible is to be interpreted like any other book, why should the biblical deity not be understood like any other deity? If the question is put as to why one should privilege and (in some way) believe in the biblical portrayal of God in the first place, and therefore undertake to spend time with and study the Bible, it is unclear from the mass of biblical commentaries and monographs of the nineteenth and twentieth centuries that an answer could be generally given with appropriate sophistication, analogous to the sophistication directed to the philological and historical study of the biblical text.

There are thus related questions. Should the Bible be studied solely as a human phenomenon whose human dimensions are the exclusive focus of interest, with no attention paid to God? Or, if Christian scholars continue to believe that the God of the Bible is, in some way, the one true God, will they offer a sufficient account of why this is warranted in relation to other deities of the ancient world in whom they do not believe—and, relatedly, discuss how the way they study the Bible is commensurate with their belief in its God?[27]

The Case Study: The *Aeneid* and the Book of Daniel

In each chapter of this book I will focus on one specific case study that raises in a detailed way some of the key issues that I am trying to discuss in a general way. There are perhaps two questions in particular that underlie this case study. First, how, if at all, does biblical content differ from the religious content of other traditions, ancient or modern? The wider issue at stake in this is, as is often put crudely, whether all religions are basically the same. Second, on what grounds, if any, should credence, in one degree or another, be given to what the biblical writers say about God

27. In excursus 1 following this chapter, I consider a nicely pointed account of this issue in the work of David Clines that is illustrative of my thesis in relation to contemporary biblical scholarship.

and life that should not equally be given to what other religious or secular traditions say about God (or god, or the gods) and life? The wider issue at stake in this has to do with why someone would believe one religious tradition and not another—and relatedly, why someone would believe any religious tradition at all.

In my overall discussion I am *not* trying to add to the literature in which scholars claim, or conversely deny, the "superiority" or "uniqueness" of biblical material in relation to other ancient material. Debates along these lines tend to be illuminating mainly about the scholars making or denying the claims, but beyond that they are usually circular and unproductive.[28] The deeper questions, which sometimes appear in skewed form in these other debates, concern the nature of the grounds (if any) whereby ancient religious and cultural traditions can be considered enduringly significant (i.e., "classics"), and the nature of the grounds (if any) whereby particular ancient traditions, of which individual texts are an expression, can today still be considered to have enduring truth content about God, humanity, and life (i.e., be "Scripture").

My approach will be to look at one particular biblical passage (initially) in relation to one particular ancient parallel, and so the exercise will necessarily be highly selective. It will, however, set some of the content of the Bible alongside part of one of the great and enduring literary classics of Western civilization. I hope it will be clear that these questions about the interpretation of particular texts and beliefs in antiquity are also questions about the status of the Bible and the possibility of faith in the biblical God today.

28. The history and nature of such debates in the modern period, primarily in relation to Israel's scriptures and ancient Near Eastern material (though the issues are hardly different in relation to the New Testament and material from the Greco-Roman world), is neatly delineated in Christopher B. Hays, *Hidden Riches: A Sourcebook for the Comparative Study of the Hebrew Bible and Ancient Near East* (Louisville: Westminster John Knox, 2014), 15–38.

Jupiter and the Romans in Aeneid 1

I turn initially to ancient Rome and the world of Augustus, the first Roman emperor. The time is the late first century BC/BCE/↓,[29] not long before the writing of the New Testament documents, and not long after the latest documents of the Old Testament, such as Daniel. This was also the world of Virgil (70–19↓), who wrote an epic poem in honor of Augustus and the incipient Roman Empire: the *Aeneid*.[30] In this poem Virgil traces the origins of Rome back to the Trojan War, made famous by Homer. Specifically, he focuses on Aeneas and other ancient heroes who survived the fall of Troy and were providentially preserved to found a new civilization in Italy.

In the story line ("the world within the text") of *Aeneid* 1, when Aeneas has been shipwrecked and appears to be in trouble, Jupiter reassures Aeneas's anxious mother, Venus, with the promise of a great destiny for her son and his descendants, the Romans.[31] Jupiter rehearses the story of Rome's origins, and in what he says of Rome and the Romans there are two keynotes. On the one hand, Jupiter bestows upon Rome unending dominion over the world:

> "On them I set no limits, space or time:
> I have granted them power, empire without end." (*Aen.*
>   1.333–34)[32]
> [*his ego nec metas rerum nec tempora pono:*
> *imperium sine fine dedi.*]

29. For the use of the symbols BC/BCE/↓ see excursus 2 following ch. 2, where I acknowledge the problems caused by the dating system BC/AD but argue that the commonly adopted BCE/CE is hardly an improvement, and so suggest a different system: to use ↓ instead of BC/BCE and ↑ instead of AD/CE.

30. Translations of the *Aeneid* abound. For this initial brief account I am using the fine rendering of Robert Fagles, *The Aeneid* (New York: Penguin, 2008). For the Latin text I use *P. Vergili Maronis Opera*, ed. R. A. B. Mynors, OCT (Oxford: Clarendon, 1969).

31. In Fagles, 1.307–55; in the Latin, 1.257–96.

32. The line numbers are from Fagles; in the Latin, 1.278–79.

On the other hand, this empire will be ruled by a descendant
of Aeneas, who will bring wars to an end and establish peace:

> "From that noble blood will arise a Trojan Caesar . . .
> Julius. . . .
> Then will the violent centuries, battles set aside,
> grow gentle, kind." (*Aen.* 1.342, 344, 348–49)[33]

The meaning of this memorable dialogue between Jupiter
and Venus, when read in relation to its context of composition
and initial use ("the world behind the text")—that is, the world
of Augustus and Virgil—would seem to be reasonably clear.
The Roman Empire should be understood to have been providentially established by the will of the sovereign deity, and the
empire's dominant role has no envisaged limit of space and time.
This victorious and enduring empire will be realized under the
leadership of a particular person, almost certainly the emperor
Augustus. Thus the Roman Empire under Augustus should be
understood as the sovereign deity's long-term gift to the world.

The Lord and the Jewish People in Daniel 7

One of the Old Testament's many famous and memorable
scenarios is found in the book of Daniel.[34] The context depicted
in the narrative framework of the book ("the world within
the text") is that of the Jewish people in exile in Babylon. The
book's particular focus is on the struggle of Daniel and three
friends, who have lost everything and been deported to an alien
land, to remain faithful to their distinctive Jewish identity and
religious allegiance, despite recurring pressures to compromise
or abandon them. After the opening narratives, there is a particularly striking visionary scenario in Daniel 7.

33. In Fagles; in the Latin, 1.286, 288, 291.
34. For English translations of the Old Testament I use the NRSV. The Hebrew
and Aramaic text is taken from *BHS*. The text of Dan. 7 is in Aramaic.

Initially Daniel sees a fearsome picture of four violent and destructive beasts, beasts that have great power over others. After this, he sees a court of judgment, presided over by an "Ancient One," who clearly represents the LORD, the God of Israel. Here the beasts lose their power, now described as dominion (Aramaic *sholtān*), and this dominion is bestowed elsewhere:

> I saw one like a human being [Aramaic "son of man"]
>   coming with the clouds of heaven.
> And he came to the Ancient One
>   and was presented before him.
> To him was given dominion [*sholtān*]
>   and glory and kingship,
> that all peoples, nations, and languages
>   should serve him.
> His dominion is an everlasting dominion [*sholtān
>   'ālam*]
>   that shall not pass away,
> and his kingship is one
>   that shall never be destroyed. (Dan. 7:13–14)

As the vision continues, it is interpreted to Daniel by one of the figures attending the Ancient One. The human being who receives universal and unending dominion in place of the beasts is seen to be symbolic of a people:

> "The holy ones of the Most High shall receive the kingdom and possess the kingdom forever—forever and ever [*'ad-'ālmā'*]." (Dan. 7:18)

These holy ones are the Jewish people.

Although the narrative setting ("the world within the text") is the life of Jewish exiles in Babylon in the sixth century↓, the most likely context of the text's composition and initial use ("the world behind the text") is the life of Jewish people in the second century↓, during their resistance to Hellenistic domination at the hands of the Syrian ruler Antiochus Epiphanes. In light of this, the book of Daniel appears to have been a kind of resistance literature, written so that second-century Jews could understand their struggles and face suffering with confidence in their ultimate vindication by their God.

Preliminary Comparison and Evaluation of Aeneid 1 and Daniel 7

For present purposes, it is the prima facie similarity between these two scenarios, in *Aeneid* 1 and in Daniel 7,[35] that is striking. It is a similarity both of terminology and of content, with four key points of likeness. In each context a sovereign deity (Jupiter, the Ancient One) bestows sovereignty on earth (*imperium, sholtān*) upon a specially favored people (Romans, Jews), a sovereignty that explicitly has no envisaged termination but is to be endlessly enduring (*sine fine, 'ad-'ālmā'*).

Two further significant similarities between the two visions should also be noted. On the one hand, each scenario shares the fact that its vision of unending dominion, at least as apparently envisaged, was not realized and has passed into history. To be sure, Roman imperial power did endure for several centuries. It lasted until the fifth century (or whenever one dates the end point of the Roman Empire—a tricky question, since the existence of the empire can be seen to extend further via Byzantium in the East and/or the "Holy Roman Empire" in the West). A Jewish dominion received some historical realization in the successful Maccabean struggle for Jewish independence. That independence, however, did not bring with it dominion over other nations, and it was terminated about a century later by Roman rule, through Pompey's conquest of Judea in 63↓. Moreover, the

---

35. I will use "*Aeneid* 1" as convenient shorthand for that portion of *Aeneid* book 1 that is under discussion here.

life of the Jewish people in their ancient homeland was largely extinguished after the Roman suppression of the Second Jewish Revolt in 135↑, with the expulsion of Jews from Jerusalem and its rebuilding as a pagan city, Aelia Capitolina.

On the other hand, the content of each vision can be seen to embody perspectives related to a major contemporary ("post-colonial") anxiety: the alignment of religion with power, in which religious appeals to the deity seem to rationalize, and seek to gain acceptance of, exercises of power that privilege and benefit the strong (and often determinedly ruthless) at the expense of others. Such anxiety is undoubtedly well warranted by all too much of human history, however much postcolonial mind-sets may become one-sided and reductive in their inter-pretation of the complex phenomenon of empires.

I will return to these visions in subsequent chapters and say more about them then. For the present I want to emphasize the similarity of the two visions (while allowing for their differ-ences) and take seriously what I consider to be a characteristi-cally modern approach to their interpretation. The scenario in the *Aeneid* would seem to be a prime embodiment of Ludwig Feuerbach's (1804–72) influential argument that accounts of deity are really a coded presentation of the ideals and aspira-tions of humanity, projected onto a big screen. It is also perhaps a good example of Émile Durkheim's (1858–1917) argument that religious beliefs, practices, and images symbolize what-ever is most important for a society's self-understanding. In the *Aeneid*, the picture of a dominant empire expresses the hopes and ideals of a militarily oriented society. Virgil puts his, and presumably Augustus's, hopes for what the Roman Empire might be into an epic narrative presided over by Jupiter. The question, then, is: Why should the vision in Daniel be treated differently from the vision in the *Aeneid*? Does it not look like some Jews were essentially doing the same as some Romans—hoping for a glorious future and ascribing it to the will of their deity, although in reality this future was not to be realized? In a word, is not talk about the divine *really* talk about *human* hopes and values? The biblical vision of God eloquently expresses the psychology and worldview of the ancients, and can be seen as a significant contributor to the historic culture and heritage of Western civilization, as Virgil has been also. But as a possible bearer of truth for the contemporary world of the twenty-first century, the biblical vision is sadly lacking. Why should the LORD's dealings with ancient Jews be understood differently from Jupiter's dealings with ancient Romans?

This is not where I want to end. But unless we begin here, we may be in danger of not engaging properly with at least some of the real challenges inherent in the question of how and why it can be meaningful and realistic for people today to believe in the God of the Bible.

EXCURSUS 1

* * * ✦ * * * ✦ * * *

Why Privilege the Biblical Portrayal of God?

An interesting example of calling into question biblical scholars' time-honored practice of privileging what the Bible says about God, without giving any justification or rationale for so doing, is David Clines's essay "Metacommentating Amos."[1] Since Clines is arguably the most influential contemporary biblical scholar in Great Britain (and is the only British scholar to have been president of the Society of Biblical Literature, the world's largest scholarly society in the field of biblical study), his voice merits attention. Although his essay is impish, it nonetheless makes a sharp point and also offers an opportunity for reflection on some of the conventions of biblical scholarship.

Clines focuses on what many scholars who work on the book of Amos do *not* say—that is, what they take for granted: "They adopt the ideology of the text regarding the existence of

---

1. David J. A. Clines, "Metacommentating Amos," in *Interested Parties: The Ideology of Writers and Readers of the Hebrew Bible*, JSOTSup 205 (Sheffield, UK: Sheffield Academic, 1995), 76–93. Another lively work, by an erstwhile colleague of Clines, that raises comparable questions in a more extended way, is Philip R. Davies's *Whose Bible Is It Anyway?* JSOTSup 204 (Sheffield, UK: Sheffield Academic, 1995). Rather than engage in detail with these and other comparable works, I have decided to concentrate on setting out my own account of many of the issues they raise, with occasional interaction as in this excursus.

God and the authenticity of the prophetic vocation," yet "they conceal from their readers that this is what they are doing."[2] They display uncritical acceptance (Clines contends) of the contestable claims found in the biblical text, but keep quiet about doing so.

Clines finds a mismatch between scholarly principle and practice. On the one hand, "the book of Amos is founded on the belief that Amos the prophet had actually been spoken to by God. This is what he claims when he says, 'Thus says Yahweh.' It is an amazing claim." On the other hand, such a claim is also "shocking": "Most of our acquaintances, we ought to recall, think that people who claim to hear voices from the sky should be locked up." Clines then observes that "commentators are hardy souls . . . not easily alarmed, and generous of spirit." For, as he goes on to ask, "how else to explain the fact that almost every textbook on Amos accepts Amos's claim, the book's ideology?"[3]

The way Clines sets things up is presumably designed to provoke. After all, even if it were the case that most people today think that those who "claim to hear voices from the sky should be locked up"—though this flippant portrayal of the issue of hearing voices in relation to mental health and public safety bears little relation to reality—the text of Amos says nothing at all about "voices from the sky." Clines's unsympathetic way of expressing the claim that God might have spoken to someone is, I imagine, designed to provoke some recognition of what is at stake in the claim that God speaks to human beings, and to make the point that for scholars to take for granted and accept without argument something so momentous is a dereliction of duty.

However, his seeming astonishment at scholars' "accept[ing] Amos' claim, the book's ideology" ignores the actual reasons— which one presumes he must in fact know well—for this schol-

2. Clines, "Metacommentating Amos," 78.
3. Clines, "Metacommentating Amos," 85.

arly practice. Amos is part of the Bible, and the Bible has been, and is, studied because of its foundationally formative role in the Jewish and Christian faiths. Christian faith (to take only the latter) has historically had enormous influence on Western culture, and it remains the largest religion in the world today. Most scholars who study the Bible would not bother to do so in the first place were it not for this history of influence into which they themselves have in some way entered. Moreover, with any work that has stood the test of time—in other words, many classics as well as the Bible—it is hardly foolish or unreasonable to go with the flow of what it says, unless there is good evidence or reason not to do so.

Interestingly, Clines does not even try to offer actual evidence that Amos was mistaken. Rather, he just reiterates in various ways the point of principle that Amos's saying it is so does not mean it really is so—which, in the abstract, is obviously true, but ignores the social nature of knowledge (about which more will be said in ch. 3), a factor that makes sense of why Christian scholars go along with what Amos says. The fact that such scholars do not declare their working assumptions does not mean that they "conceal" them; rightly or wrongly, they simply share the common scholarly predilection for not focusing on metaquestions but rather working within accepted scholarly conventions. I take it, however, that the real focus of Clines's critique is the tendency of Christian biblical scholars simply to assume the reality of God in a contemporary culture where such an assumption is no longer appropriate because Christian faith is no longer generally held. As Clines puts it in one place: "Any reader who thinks that such an analysis of the scholar's religious commitment is hypercritical might like to consider how the sentences would sound if we substituted Zeus for Yahweh."[4] To which it is hard not to respond with: quite so.

---

4. Clines, "Metacommentating Amos," 88.

Clines sets all this up in a sharp way that risks weakening his thesis. He consistently polarizes "being critical" and "giving assent," with no allowance for the fact that, generally speaking, scholars devote themselves to a lifetime's study of something because they think it important or worthwhile or true, and because they may love their subject. He can hardly be proposing that the factor that brings people to their scholarly work, their predisposition in favor of what they are studying, has to be discarded when they set to work. The point is not to abandon one's predisposition, but *to learn to discipline it*. Nonetheless, his key insight is still surely valid. Too many scholars of the Bible have allowed the fundamental rationale for their privileging of the Bible and of its content to drop out of sight. They privilege the Bible and the biblical portrayal of God, and yet, at least in their scholarly work, offer little or no account of why they do so and treat their working assumptions as somehow self-evident. Clines's challenge is clear and still too little addressed by biblical scholars, despite the growing recognition of the ways in which ideologies, beliefs, interests, and locations affect scholarship.

Thus the question remains: On what grounds, if any, is it appropriate to privilege the Bible and the biblical account of God in the world of today?

2

Approaching the Bible

Thus far I have sought to pose a problem: How can the classic Christian understanding of the Bible as "the most valuable thing that this world affords," as a source of ultimate truth and wisdom about God and humanity, be meaningful in a disenchanted age? In Western culture, God and theological thinking have been pushed to the margins. The Bible is no longer the privileged lens for viewing the world, but rather just a possibly interesting object within it. The working assumption of many Christian scholars—that in their scholarly work they should interpret the Bible "like any other book"—has usually been accompanied by a lack of interest in clarifying in what ways (if any) the Bible is *un*like any other book. They have continued to assume the in-some-way-privileged position of the Bible. But that assumption belongs to a Christendom that has passed away. Indeed, many people in contemporary culture have become casually dismissive of the Bible, and regularly, in one way or another, raise the question "Why should I/we/anyone bother with the Bible in today's world?"

How might progress be made? A first step (to state the obvious) is to recognize the legitimacy of reading the Bible in secular as well as in religious ways. At least some people do take the Bible seriously, and they do so for entirely, or at least largely, nonreligious reasons. Although my own approach relates to the Bible's significance for faith in God, this needs to be contextualized in relation to other possible approaches. Moreover, given the enormous gains in understanding the nature of the biblical text and its content that have come from the last two centuries of biblical scholarship, a faith-oriented approach can be kept alert and honest by attending to insights and questions from other approaches.

At the risk of oversimplifying, I propose a typology of three primary ways of reading the Bible: as history, as classic, and as Scripture. In this chapter I briefly sketch out the first two of these, which will further develop some of the points already made in chapter 1. I will also return to the case study of *Aeneid* 1 and Daniel 7 and offer a fuller reading of the texts in a way that illustrates something of the obvious value of reading that may be independent of religious concerns. In chapters 3 and 4, however, where I will set out something of what it means to read the biblical documents as Christian Scripture, I will also suggest that my seemingly straightforward initial reading of *Aeneid* 1 and Daniel 7 may in fact require a more nuanced and differentiated account of the overall interpretive task.

On Taking the Bible Seriously

The Bible as Ancient History

The first approach is to view and study the Bible as a source of ancient literature, history, and religion. To read the Bible thus is comparable to reading the literary remains of ancient Greece, Rome, Egypt, Mesopotamia, or any other ancient culture around the world. Such ancient literature can be potentially fascinating to those who become interested in it and perhaps develop a taste for it. This kind of reading can be done without any concern for whether the Bible contains enduring truth, such as has characterized the understanding of the Bible by Jews and Christians. The material is interesting because it has survived and gives insights into human cultures other than our own. Just as Mount Everest attracts mountain climbers, one can want to engage with the biblical material simply because it is there; and the serious study of ancient literature can sometimes be the intellectual equivalent of taking an exploratory trip to another part of the world and immersing oneself in, and learning about and being existentially enriched by, a new and unfamiliar place.

This approach may be characterized as *the Bible as ancient history*. In such a context, the study of the Bible in principle includes any and every document and artifact of ancient Israel and the early Christian movement in their wider worlds. The specific boundaries formed by the biblical canon have little or no significance in themselves, beyond the convenience with which the canonical collection makes numerous ancient documents readily available. Historians routinely ignore the boundaries of the biblical canon. One primary reason for this is that the canon recontextualizes documents in a composite literary collection that is other than their context of origin, and so might be misleading for understanding that context of origin. Engagement with the biblical documents with the questions and priorities of ancient history is the form that much modern scholarly study has in fact taken, or at least aspired to take, and is regularly designated by the already-noted shorthand phrase "the historical-critical approach."

Focusing on the Bible as ancient history was the primary way in which biblical study became a discipline independent of Christian theology in the modern world. As already noted, it was first programmatically proposed in the seventeenth century by Spinoza in his *Tractatus Theologico-Politicus* of 1670.[1] Spinoza proposed it precisely so as to diminish the Bible's significance in the contemporary world. If the Bible is only ancient history, it need not excite people in the way that arguments about it were exciting Spinoza's contemporaries, when European states and sociopolitical life were still religiously defined. Such biblically derived religious self-definition was problematic in many ways, not least because of the divisions and confrontations between Protestants, Roman Catholics, and Jews; and it was also personally problematic for Spinoza himself. In due course others followed Spinoza's lead. One landmark moment, at least in retrospect, was Johann Gabler's inaugural address at the University of Altdorf in 1787, with its illuminating title "An Oration on the Proper Distinction between Biblical and Dogmatic Theology and the Specific Objectives of Each."[2] The distinction between biblical theology and dogmatic theology became (whatever Gabler's own intentions) a distinction between reading the biblical documents historically—that is, in terms of their meaning in their context of origin—and reading them dogmatically in relation to the concerns of continuing Christian thought and practice. Over time, the essence of Spinoza's proposal to read the biblical documents as ancient history independent of subsequent theology became widely adopted and came to constitute what is now called the historical-critical approach.

This historicizing of biblical study meant that in principle little, if anything, was distinctively religious or theological about it, for the point was precisely to expel theological arguments and dogmatic assumptions from the discipline. Or rather, doing "theology" in a biblical context came to mean offering an account of the history and nature of religious thought and practice in ancient Israel and/or the early church. But such an account would not in principle be different from accounts of religious thought and practice in any context—pagan, Hindu, Muslim, New Age, or whatever. Such religious material could be interesting, and understanding it better could be a contribution to human knowledge. But questions about whether a student should believe or live in accordance with the content of what is studied, and if so how, are no longer necessary questions; and, at least in secular institutions of education, such questions are generally seen to be inappropriate and out of place.

1. See Elwes, *Benedict de Spinoza*. Chapter 7, "Of the Interpretation of Scripture," offers a useful summary statement of Spinoza's thesis. See, for example, the citation I have already given in ch. 1 (above, p. 25).

2. See John Sandys-Wunsch and Laurence Eldredge, "J. P. Gabler and the Distinction between Biblical and Dogmatic Theology: Translation, Commentary, and Discussion of His Originality," *Scottish Journal of Theology* 33 (1980): 133–58.

Historians are unsurprisingly nervous about apparently historical arguments regarding the reliability and accuracy of biblical content that appear
to be motivated by religious/theological concerns. For then there is a danger
that the evidence may not be fairly evaluated, but rather prejudged. To be
sure, the difficulties here can arise in many contexts other than theological
ones. The underlying issue is that the more the history of an event or person
matters to those discussing it (which is often the case with content that
touches on human identity and self-understanding, whether familial or
national or religious), the harder it is not to allow one's own interest to affect
and perhaps skew one's handling of the issue; though it is also possible that
one's interest might enhance one's handling. Nonetheless, it is not hard to
grasp the basic principle that, as with a judge and a jury at a trial, one's own
preferences should not be allowed to override the accurate establishment,
as far as is possible, of what actually happened. Therefore, some distance
between historical arguments and faith claims can regularly be salutary.

In practice, the majority of modern historical-critical work
on the Bible has been done by scholars who, like Benjamin
Jowett, have also been believers; they have seen no intrinsic opposition between historical-critical study and faith. Such study
regularly receives a twofold justification. On the one hand,
scholars need to understand what kind of material the ancient
biblical documents really are, and what they are really saying, so
that their true meaning and significance can be rightly grasped;
belief in relation to the Bible needs to be based on as accurate
an understanding as possible of its content. On the other hand,
scholars need to be free from constraint or inhibition so that
they can with integrity follow the philological and historical
evidence wherever it may lead. In this way, certain traditional
and time-honored understandings may in fact need to be recognized as unwarranted, and scholars will only recognize this if
in certain respects they are able to bracket out aspects of their
faith while they work. Both reasons have a certain self-evident
value. Thus, churches that recognize the Bible as authoritative
generally expect to be enriched by such work, even if its value
may not immediately be apparent. But despite these reasons

for believing scholars to practice historical-critical study of the Bible, my present concern is that historical interest in, and study of, the Bible is a mode of study that can in principle be independent of faith. The Bible can be studied like other documents of ancient history—in other words, "like any other book."[3]

The Bible as Cultural Classic

Second in my typology of approaches is an interest in viewing and studying the Bible as a cultural artifact of enormous historical, and to some extent continuing, influence within Western civilization: *the Bible as a classic*. This can take a number of distinct, though not unrelated, forms.

First is the study of the Bible as a source of sayings, images, and understandings that are expressed in the literature, art, architecture, music, and general life of European and European-influenced cultures. Since for so much of Western history the content of the Bible was (in one way or another) part of common knowledge, it can be hard to understand Western culture without being familiar with the biblical content that was constantly presupposed and expressed within it. In this sense even Richard Dawkins has no problem with advocating the need to know the Bible. As he puts it: "The main reason the English Bible needs to be part of our education is that it is a major source book for literary culture" (to which, unsurprisingly, he immediately adds: "The same applies to the legends of the Greek and Roman gods, and we learn about them without being asked to believe in them").[4] This approach, which might be called *the Bible as cultural source*, is exemplified in the growth of courses on the Bible for students of English literature, simply to familiarize students with biblical content.

3. I have not discussed the many methods that cluster under the umbrella of a historical-critical approach, for there are so many discussions available that they need no addition here.

4. Dawkins, *God Delusion*, 341.

Second is a striking contemporary growth of interest in the reception history of the biblical documents down the centuries. Here the focus remains on the Bible as Bible in the first instance, rather than on the wider culture. However, instead of studying how the Bible arose and was understood in its context of origin, attention is given to the many and various ways in which the Bible has been understood and used—in other words, the interest is in the Bible as generative of its own continuing history among its readers. For example, how was the book of Revelation understood by sixteenth-century Protestants, or how was Isaiah understood by Handel? This approach is analogous to trends in the study of Greek and Roman classics, with a comparable shift of interest from how the texts arose to what people have made of them. In place of a common nineteenth-century dismissiveness towards the history of interpretation as a history of misinterpretation, there is a potentially appreciative openness to the variety of ways in which resonant texts can be read. This is an approach to *the Bible as source of a continuing reception history*.

A third approach is what might be called *the Bible as cultural heritage*, which envisages not just knowing about the Bible but perhaps even participating in dimensions of contemporary culture that are still shaped by the Bible. Again Richard Dawkins, in significant ways a cultural conservative, has no problem with this:

> Of course we can retain a sentimental loyalty to the cultural and literary traditions of, say, Judaism, Anglicanism or Islam, and even participate in religious rituals such as marriages and funerals, without buying into the supernatural beliefs that historically went along with those traditions. We can give up belief in God while not losing touch with a treasured heritage.[5]

5. Dawkins, *God Delusion*, 344.

Certain glossy and well-illustrated books about the Bible, its world, and its influence seem designed for this kind of approach, in which the Bible becomes something that one might peruse in much the same spirit as one might visit a medieval cathedral. Alternatively, some contemporary scholars are interested in identifying the ways in which biblical content and imagery continue to inform and shape certain dimensions of contemporary culture, though these scholars usually show little or no interest in the possible enduring truth of that content.[6]

Finally, one can include the category of *the Bible as a literary classic of the human condition*. Here there can be an appreciative interest in how the Bible probes human life in the world in ways that can be profound, moving, and suggestive. However, the Bible is understood to be comparable to the great literary classics rather than a sacred text or revelation of God. Readers can recognize depth and resonance in the biblical documents in an entirely unpredictable way, and be enriched thereby. Such recognition and enrichment need not entail commitment to a belief in the reality of the God of whom the Bible speaks, membership in a church or synagogue, or certain of the life practices that, on the basis of the Bible, Jews and Christians have commended through the ages, such as prayer or financial giving or self-denial (though of course these might come about as unanticipated results).

A distinctive account of this approach to the Bible is offered by D. H. Lawrence in the course of a discussion of the novel and his own work as a novelist. Lawrence says (writing in a context before the raising of consciousness in matters of gender in language):

6. An interesting representative example is *Rethinking Biblical Literacy*, ed. Katie Edwards (New York: Bloomsbury T&T Clark, 2015). The concern of the various fascinating essays is to show how biblical content is picked up in popular culture and the media. Questions about how biblical knowledge might relate to the acquiring or deepening of faith in God do not feature.

Now I absolutely flatly deny that I am a soul, or a body, or a mind, or an intelligence, or a brain, or a nervous system, or a bunch of glands, or any of the rest of these bits of me. The whole is greater than the part. And therefore, I, who am man alive, am greater than my soul, or spirit, or mind, or consciousness, or anything else that is merely a part of me. I am a man, and alive. I am man alive, and as long as I can, I intend to go on being man alive.

For this reason I am a novelist. And being a novelist, I consider myself superior to the saint, the scientist, the philosopher, and the poet, who are all great masters of different bits of man alive, but never get the whole hog.

The novel is the one bright book of life. Books are not life. They are only tremulations on the ether. But the novel as a tremulation can make the whole man alive tremble. Which is more than poetry, philosophy, science, or any other book-tremulation can do.

The novel is the book of life. In this sense, the Bible is a great confused novel. You may say, it is about God. But it is really about man alive. Adam, Eve, Sarai, Abraham, Isaac, Jacob, Samuel, David, Bath-Sheba, Ruth, Esther, Solomon, Job, Isaiah, Jesus, Mark, Judas, Paul, Peter: what is it but man alive, from start to finish? Man alive, not mere bits. Even the Lord is another man alive, in a burning bush, throwing the tablets of stone at Moses' head. . . .[7]

I do ask that the whole of me shall tremble in its wholeness, some time or other. And this, of course, must happen in me, living.

But as far as it can happen from a communication, it can only happen when a whole novel communicates itself to me. The Bible—but *all* the Bible—and Homer, and Shakespeare: these are the supreme old novels. These are all things to all men. Which means that in their wholeness they affect the whole man alive, which is the man himself, beyond any part of him.[8]

7. One wonders which particular passage(s) Lawrence had in mind for this last point!

8. D. H. Lawrence, "Why the Novel Matters," in *Selected Literary Criticism*, ed. Anthony Beal (London: Heinemann, 1956), 104–5.

Lawrence (apparently not a modest man!) was not interested in promoting faith. But he still wanted a serious and substantial engagement with the content of the Bible as a whole, and considered such engagement to be enriching.

One major contemporary example of an approach to the Bible as a literary classic of the human condition is the work of Robert Alter, a professor of Hebrew and comparative literature who is producing a fresh annotated translation of the Hebrew Scriptures and who wrote a groundbreaking book on narrative in the Hebrew Scriptures.[9] Alter's work seems designed to reestablish this material as a major Jewish contribution to Western culture. He presents the biblical material as having the resonance and depth and enduring interest of all great literature, but without any apparent interest in its possible appropriation for trusting God and living faithfully today.

This rough typology of approaches is heuristic rather than exhaustive. For example, I am not aware of any close equivalent for the Bible to the wide-ranging work that Mary Beard does with the literature and history of ancient Rome, work that would come under all these subdivisions (except perhaps the first).[10] But that may just mean that interest in the Bible, as in the classics generally, can take many forms.

In all this, my concern is to make the basic point that it is entirely possible to take the Bible seriously, and to benefit from so doing, without taking it religiously—and to offer a provisional map of some of the many different ways of doing so.

9. Representative of Alter's weighty oeuvre are *The Art of Biblical Narrative* (London: Allen & Unwin, 1981), *Canon and Creativity: Modern Writing and the Authority of Scripture* (New Haven: Yale University Press, 2000), and *The Five Books of Moses: A Translation with Commentary* (New York and London: Norton, 2004).

10. In addition to her recent *SPQR: A History of Ancient Rome* (London: Profile, 2015), Mary Beard ranges fascinatingly between antiquity and modernity in her reviews and essays collected in *Confronting the Classics: Traditions, Adventures and Innovations* (London: Profile, 2013). She also appears regularly on television as an informed and accessible interpreter of Roman history and culture.

Such approaches are compatible with a believing approach to the Bible, and indeed should be used to inform one. Nonetheless, their raison d'être is independent of questions of faith.

The relationship between approaches to the Bible that are independent of faith and those that are related to faith can be complex and can take many forms. Accounts of the value of reading the Bible as ancient history and/or cultural classic are not infrequently accompanied by rhetoric to the effect that only by reading the Bible thus—that is, without religious faith commitments—can one really read it well. Biblical scholar Robert Carroll opposes "the ecclesiastical captivity of the Bible . . . the theological Colditz to which the Bible has been condemned" to the positive though unpredictable results when "the imagination is let loose on the imaginative productions of human culture."[11] Comparably, literary scholar Simon Loveday laments that "the Bible has been made into an instrument of divine tyranny, but like all great powers of culture, it is a work of the human imagination, and artists have always recognised that. Properly understood it celebrates our recapture of our own imaginings."[12] Of course, if one reckons that God is no more than a product of the human imagination, then approaches that celebrate the human imagination and set aside the debilitating historic structures, practices, and understandings of Christian faith can be considered liberating. But for those who do not share that working assumption, or at least may be uncertain about it, the reality of what is necessary to read religious literature well may be more complex and challenging: still imaginative, but by no means solely imaginative.

On a different level, the relationship between ancient-historical, cultural-classic, and faith-oriented approaches to the Bible can be complex in educational establishments, where for students and teachers there can sometimes be clashes and mismatches of expectations. Those whose reasons for studying the Bible are faith-related may encounter an agenda with little or no interest in issues of faith and theology; and students with no religious interests may encounter the opposite problem. There are thus difficult questions: Who sets which agenda of study in any context? Which questions are asked, and why, and for what purpose?[13] Also, why should educational

11. Robert P. Carroll, *Wolf in the Sheepfold: The Bible as a Problem for Christianity* (London: SPCK, 1991), xi, 146.

12. Simon Loveday, *The Bible for Grown-Ups: A New Look at the Good Book* (London: Icon, 2016), 259.

13. Some of the issues here are interestingly discussed in a preliminary way by Dale B. Martin in *Pedagogy of the Bible: An Analysis and Proposal* (Louisville: Westminster John Knox, 2008).

establishments, unless explicitly Christian, devote resources to the study of the Bible anyway? And, if they do, should the Bible be located elsewhere than ancient history or cultural studies?

There are also questions about appropriate terminology for speaking of the two Testaments of the Christian Bible, since nomenclature and approach are clearly related. The question is most acute for the first part of the Christian canon: "Old Testament" (a Christian term), "Tanakh" (a Jewish term), "Hebrew Bible" or "First Testament" (supposedly religiously neutral terms), or what? But it applies also to the second part: "New Testament," "Apostolic Writings," "Second Testament," or what? Different names relate to different contexts and purposes within which and for which the material is approached.[14]

Finally, there are questions about how far one should continue to speak of "the Bible" at all in contexts that seek to prescind from the continuing life of Judaism and Christianity. For the canon is a construct of ancient and contemporary Jews and Christians that has no obvious validity outside a Jewish and Christian frame of reference (on which, see further below in ch. 3). These questions tend to be sharper for ancient-historical study than for cultural-classic study, for in the latter the Bible qua Bible has generally been a given.

For the present I simply note some of these difficulties without seeking to engage with them.

The Case Study: A Fuller Reading of *Aeneid* 1 and Daniel 7

Having thus prepared the way for advancing my own constructive thesis in the following chapters, I want to turn again to the case study of *Aeneid* 1 and Daniel 7 that runs through each chapter of this book.

To the best of my knowledge, this particular comparison between *Aeneid* 1 and Daniel 7, though obviously known to scholars, does not have as much discussion and literature around it as one might perhaps expect. Recent postcolonial interests in empire and imperial rhetoric have led to some attention to these passages, usually in a history-of-ideas way in terms of

14. A good recent discussion is Stephen Chapman's "Collections, Canons, and Communities," in *The Cambridge Companion to the Hebrew Bible / Old Testament*, ed. Stephen B. Chapman and Marvin A. Sweeney (New York: Cambridge University Press, 2016), 28–54, esp. 36–41.

respective Roman and Jewish imperial and counterimperial ideologies, and sometimes with interest in the possible mutual awareness of, or influence between, these ideologies.[15] But I am not aware of any precedent for an in-depth comparison and evaluation of *Aeneid* 1 and Daniel 7 such as I will attempt in this book.

In line with the discussion so far, I will expand my brief reference to these passages in the previous chapter with a fuller account of them within the categories of ancient history, with a general working assumption that both texts are in some way cultural classics. I hope this will both illustrate the interpretive insights that come from a disciplined historical approach to classic texts and also provide a better basis for the comparison and evaluation that will follow in subsequent chapters.

The Narrative Context and Content of Jupiter's Words in Aeneid 1

The story line ("the world within the text") of book 1 of the *Aeneid* depicts some of the anguished wanderings of Aeneas, who has escaped from Troy after its capture by the Greeks (courtesy of the original Trojan horse) and is sailing for Italy but is unable to reach it. He is up against the hostility of Juno, the sister and wife of Jupiter, the supreme and sovereign deity. Juno is unremittingly opposed to the Trojan people for various reasons, most famously because of the snub to her beauty delivered by Paris, one of the sons of Priam, the last king of Troy. Juno's latest hostile move is the summoning of a storm that shipwrecks Aeneas and his fleet on the coast of Libya. After Aeneas's shipwreck, his divine mother, Venus, who is anxious

15. See, e.g., Ekkehard W. Stegemann, "Coexistence and Transformation: Reading the Politics of Identity in Romans in an Imperial Context," in *Reading Paul in Context: Explorations in Identity Formation; Essays in Honour of William S. Campbell*, ed. Kathy Ehrensperger and J. Brian Tucker (London: T&T Clark, 2010), esp. 6, 7, 21, 23. A valuable general discussion of empire and power in relation to biblical perspectives is Christopher Bryan's *Render to Caesar: Jesus, the Early Church, and the Roman Superpower* (New York: Oxford University Press, 2005).

for her son, approaches Jupiter and expresses her fear that Aeneas's glorious future, which she had understood to be Jupiter's will for him, appears to be in jeopardy:

> "What great crime did Aeneas and the Trojans
> Commit against you? They have died and died,
> But in the whole world found no Italy.
> You promised that the circling years would draw
> Teucer's new lineage from them, Romans, chieftains,
> To rule an empire on the land and sea.
> Father, what new thought turns you from this pur-
>   pose?" (*Aen.* 1.231–37)[16]

Jupiter responds to this plea with words of reassurance. The glorious future for Aeneas and his descendants for which Venus longs is indeed assured:

> "Take heart—no one will touch the destiny
> Of your people. You will see Lavinium
> In its promised walls, and raise your brave Aeneas
> To the stars. No new thoughts change my purposes."
>   (*Aen.* 1.257–60)

Indeed, Jupiter underlines this reassurance by revealing the future, and unfolding a destiny that is sure to be realized:

> "But since you suffer, I will tell the future,
> Opening to the light fate's secret book." (*Aen.* 1.261–62)

Initially, Aeneas will reach Italy, defeat his enemies there, and build a settlement where he will rule:

16. For this fuller reading of *Aeneid* 1 I will use the exceptional recent rendering of Sarah Ruden, *The Aeneid / Vergil* (New Haven and London: Yale University Press, 2008), which not only is lucid and expressive poetry in itself but also, remarkably, manages to retain the same number of lines in English as in the Latin—a feat which will best be appreciated by those who have worked at translation themselves.

> "In Italy your son will crush a fierce race
> In a great war. With the Rutulians beaten,
> Three winters and three summers he'll shape walls
> And warrior customs, as he reigns in Latium." (*Aen.*
> 1.263–66)

The focus then shifts to Aeneas's descendants. His son Ascanius (who will also be known as Iulus) will rule in his turn and will build Alba Longa, where for three centuries his dynasty will continue to rule, until a fateful moment of descent through the female line:

> ". . . until Ilia, royal priestess,
> Conceives twin boys by Mars and gives them birth.
> And the wolf's nursling (glad to wear brown wolfskin),
> Romulus, will then lead the race and found
> The walls of Mars for Romans—named for him." (*Aen.*
> 1.273–77)

The famous story of Romulus and Remus being suckled by a wolf is briefly alluded to, so as to arrive at the moment when Romulus gives his name to a warrior city and people: Rome and the Romans. The destiny that Jupiter has in store for this people is simple and clear:

> "For them I will not limit time or space.
> Their rule will have no end." (*Aen.* 1.278–79)
> [*his ego nec metas rerum nec tempora pono*:
> *imperium sine fine dedi.*]

Present difficulties caused by Juno's hostility and opposition will in due course pass away and make no difference to this destiny:

> "Even hard Juno,
> Who terrorizes land and sea and sky,
> Will change her mind and join me as I foster

> The Romans in their togas, the world's masters.
> I have decreed it." (*Aen.* 1.279–83)

Victories will come to the Romans, including victories over those who had conquered Troy, the Greeks. From this resurgent and all-conquering line of Trojan descent, one particular figure will emerge who will carry that second name given to Aeneas's son, Ascanius/Iulus:

> "The noble Trojan line will give us Caesar—
> A Julian name passed down from the great Iulus—
> With worldwide empire, glory heaven-high." (*Aen.*
>   1.286–88)

So triumphant will this Caesar, this Julius, be that he will usher in a new and better age of peace and the rule of law on earth:

> "Then wars will end, cruel history grow gentle.
> Vesta, old Faith, and Quirinus, with Remus
> His twin, will make the laws. Tight locks of iron
> Will close War's grim gates." (*Aen.* 1.291–94)

And on this note, Jupiter concludes his words to Venus, and the narrative context shifts back to Aeneas's situation on the Libyan coast.

Comparable content also appears later in the *Aeneid*, in the context of Aeneas's visit to the underworld in book 6. Here he encounters his father, Anchises, who, not unlike Jupiter, offers an overview of Roman history from its beginnings up to Virgil's own day. Although the voice of Anchises is not as intrinsically weighty as the voice of Jupiter, the fact that Anchises is the father of Aeneas and is in the privileged underworld realm of Elysium means that his words too paint an authoritative picture. Among other things, Anchises says to Aeneas:

> "But Romans, don't forget that world dominion
> Is your great craft: peace, and then peaceful customs;
> Sparing the conquered, striking down the haughty."
> (*Aen.* 6.851–53)
> [*tu regere imperio populos, Romane, memento*
> (*hae tibi erunt artes*), *pacique imponere morem,*
> *parcere subiectis et debellare superbos.*]

Jupiter's words, together with those of Anchises, offer a majestic vision. The history of Rome is to lead up to two great and conjoined goals. On the one hand, there is to be an unending empire, an empire with a moral vision of peace, mercy, the rule of law, and the overthrow of the haughty. On the other hand, there is to be a particular climactic figure through whom the goal of the vision will be realized: a Caesar named Julius.

The Aeneid *in the Context of Virgil and Augustus*

Probably the first question to ask, as we turn to "the world behind the text," the context of composition and initial use, concerns the identity of this Caesar through whom Roman dominion is to be realized.

The precise identity of this Julius Caesar is in fact open to dispute, as there are two candidates. The first is the figure known to history as Julius Caesar—the brilliant soldier who crossed the Rubicon and established himself as "dictator" in Rome in a way that heralded the transition from republic to empire, but who was assassinated by Brutus and others on the Ides of March in 44↓. The second is the figure known to history as Augustus. Known as Octavian in his early life, he was adopted as heir by Julius Caesar. He was victorious in the civil war that followed Caesar's assassination, and he became the first emperor in the republic-now-become-empire. A case can be made for either of these figures as the Julius Caesar in Jupiter's unfolding of Roman destiny. But insofar as Augustus was Virgil's patron and alive at the time of Virgil's writing, and was the one for whom yet more of a glorious destiny seemed still to be waiting, he is surely the more likely figure in the poem. With him Jupiter's survey of the history of Rome from its earliest beginnings comes right up to date.

Admittedly, the precise relationship between Virgil and Augustus is not in fact well known. There are ancient biographies of Virgil, but they are all from a time subsequent to, rather than contemporary with, what they depict.[17] Nonetheless, some clear lines emerge, and there is a plausible picture of close links between the two figures: Augustus writes to Virgil to inquire about the progress of his epic, Augustus is an appreciative audience as Virgil reads out selections of his work, and it is Augustus who overrules Virgil's reported deathbed request that his unfinished manuscript be burned. But although it makes good sense to see Virgil as a mouthpiece for Augustus's aspirations, a little caution still remains appropriate.

In terms of the *Aeneid* as a whole, two closely related questions may be asked: In what ways does Aeneas prefigure Augustus? And to what degree is the portrayal of Aeneas positive, and to what degree is it ambivalent or even negative? The clear tones of Jupiter's speech have to be set alongside an often complex and ambiguous depiction of events and persons elsewhere in the poem. Much of this ambiguity may obviously relate to the intrinsic imaginative quality of the story within Virgil's poetry, which would be diminished if it were a mere mouthpiece for fashionable politics, an apologia for the Augustan principate. But that might not be the sole reason. Not all Romans welcomed the new empire that Augustus introduced, in which the forms of the republic were retained but power was relocated; and criticism would need to be expressed cautiously for prudential

---

17. A useful introductory account is Fabio Stok's "The Life of Vergil before Donatus," in *A Companion to Vergil's* Aeneid *and Its Tradition*, ed. Joseph Farrell and Michael C. J. Putnam (Chichester, UK: Wiley-Blackwell, 2010), 107–20.

reasons (to speak freely, as Cicero did not long before, could cost one one's life). So it cannot simply be assumed that positive notes on the lips of Jupiter express Virgil's own priorities.[18]

> This ambivalence is nicely portrayed in Mary Beard's recent *SPQR: A History of Ancient Rome*. On the one hand, she says, "Augustus to all intents and purposes had writers such as Virgil and Horace on his payroll, and the work they produced offers a memorable and eloquent image of a new golden age for Rome and its empire, with Augustus centre stage. 'I have given them empire without limit' (*imperium sine fine*), Jupiter prophesies for the Romans in Virgil's *Aeneid*." On the other hand, she also says that "even Virgil's *Aeneid*, the epic poem sponsored by the emperor himself, prompts troubling questions. The figure of Aeneas, Augustus' mythical ancestor and clearly intended to be some reflection of him, is a decidedly unstraightforward hero. . . . The final scene of the poem, in which Aeneas, now established in Italy, allows his rage to triumph as he brutally kills an enemy who has surrendered, has always been an unsettling conclusion. Such ambivalences . . . continue to raise questions about Virgil's relationship with his patron and the Augustan regime."[19]

Nonetheless, even if Virgil's poetic vision relates somewhat obliquely, rather than straightforwardly, to the political world of his day, one can hardly come away from the poem without a strong sense of the Roman destiny to rule others, a destiny being realized in Virgil's own day when Augustus was at the helm. The imaginative depiction of Jupiter and his bequest of unlimited rule reflects and promotes Virgil's vision of Rome.

The Narrative Context and Content of the Ancient One's Words in Daniel 7

Although one might not be able to claim that Daniel 7 plays a role within the Old Testament comparable to the role that

18. The literary and historical complexities of Virgil's situation are interestingly discussed by R. J. Tarrant in "Poetry and Power: Virgil's Poetry in Contemporary Context," in *The Cambridge Companion to Virgil*, ed. Charles Martindale (Cambridge: Cambridge University Press, 1997), 169–87.

19. Beard, *SPQR*, 355, 376–77.

Jupiter's speech to Venus plays in the *Aeneid*, it is nonetheless widely recognized to be a passage of major importance, both in itself and in terms of its subsequent history.

The narrative context ("the world within the text") of the book of Daniel is the captivity of the people of Jerusalem and Judah, who have been forcibly taken into exile in Babylon by King Nebuchadnezzar in the sixth century↓. The historical background is portrayed in 2 Kings 25 and elsewhere in the Old Testament.

The first half of Daniel presents narratives about Daniel and three companions, who are among the exiled Jews in Babylon. It tells of their courage and faithfulness to their Jewish identity in the face of pressures to conform to a different, and often hostile, culture. But in chapter 7, the angle of vision changes (although the use of Aramaic, as from 2:4 onwards, continues).[20] Hitherto, Daniel has been a character spoken about by the narrator in the third person. Here, although initially (v. 1) Daniel is spoken about by the narrator as previously, he himself becomes the speaking voice, and this first-person portrayal persists for the whole chapter—indeed, for the rest of the book. The lead character becomes the narrator.

> In the first year of King Belshazzar of Babylon, Daniel had a dream and visions of his head as he lay in bed. Then he wrote down the dream: I, Daniel, saw in my vision by night . . . (Dan. 7:1–2)

Previously in the book, Babylonian kings have had dreams, and Daniel has interpreted them. Now Daniel himself has a dream and, as will be seen, he too will need someone else to interpret it.

20. The use of both Hebrew and Aramaic in the composition of Daniel—Hebrew from 1:1–2:4a and 8:1–12:13, but Aramaic from 2:4b–7:28—is an enduring puzzle that need not detain us here.

> [I saw] the four winds of heaven stirring up the great sea, and four great beasts came up out of the sea, different from one another. (Dan. 7:2–3)

The sea is an image with mythic resonance, suggestive of mysterious dimensions of reality that may be productive of evil and resistant to the sovereign God—as in the vision of the new heaven and new earth at the climax of the book of Revelation, when "the sea was no more" (Rev. 21:1). So beasts that arise from the sea are unlikely to bode well.

> The first was like a lion and had eagles' wings. Then, as I watched, its wings were plucked off, and it was lifted up from the ground and made to stand on two feet like a human being; and a human mind was given to it. (Dan. 7:4)

The lion is a natural image of fierce strength (and Daniel has already faced lions in the immediately preceding narrative). If initially the lion has eagles' wings so as to be a fabulous monster with a great range on the ground and in the air, its transformation into a human-like figure brings it closer to the known world. Although the loss of wings can be read as weakening the lion, the depiction perhaps suggests a creature that retains its fierce animal qualities even while its new human form and mind enable it to know how to interact with humans in recognizable ways; thus it can more readily deceive and ensnare them.

> Another beast appeared, a second one, that looked like a bear. It was raised up on one side, had three tusks [or ribs] in its mouth among its teeth and was told, "Arise, devour many bodies!" After this, as I watched, another appeared, like a leopard. The beast had four wings of a bird on its back and four heads; and dominion [*sholtān*] was given to it. After this I saw in the visions by night a fourth beast, terrifying and dreadful and exceedingly strong. It had great iron teeth and was devouring, breaking in pieces,

and stamping what was left with its feet. It was different from
all the beasts that preceded it, and it had ten horns. (Dan. 7:5–7)

One beast tears apart its prey, whose remains are apparently
still visible between the beast's teeth. The leopard-like creature
with wings can range widely, and so has widespread power
("dominion"). Behind these creatures lies some further power
(unspecified), which commissions both beasts to do what they
do. Then a fourth beast appears, consuming and crushing, perhaps finishing off those who had escaped the previous beasts.
The overall depiction is perhaps indicative of the problem that
to speak of horror and terror, as also to speak of wonder and
joy, rapidly outruns the resources of regular vocabulary, and
so readers/hearers must use their imaginations.

The fourth beast, however, is also characterized by the large
number of its horns, a feature that attracts Daniel's attention:

> I was considering the horns, when another horn appeared, a
> little one coming up among them; to make room for it, three
> of the earlier horns were plucked up by the roots. There were
> eyes like human eyes in this horn, and a mouth speaking ar-
> rogantly. (Dan. 7:8)

The horns are not only numerous, but there is movement among
them as a new horn appears and, although initially only small,
rapidly displaces some of the others. This new horn remains
in nonhuman form, but if it has human eyes and an ability
not only to speak but to speak arrogantly, then it would appear to symbolize a reality that is part bestial and part human;
moreover, through arrogance, it apparently claims supremacy
particularly for itself.

At this moment in the dream, the scene suddenly and abruptly
shifts from a stormy sea and fearsome beasts to a royal court
(and the language also appears to shift from prose to poetry).

> As I watched,
> thrones were set in place,
>   and an Ancient One [Aramaic "an Ancient of
>   Days"] took his throne,
> his clothing was white as snow,
>   and the hair of his head like pure wool;
> his throne was fiery flames,
>   and its wheels were burning fire.
> A stream of fire issued
>   and flowed out from his presence.
> A thousand thousands served him,
>   and ten thousand times ten thousand stood attend-
>   ing him.
> The court sat in judgment,
>   and the books were opened. (Dan. 7:9–10)

It is an oddity of the book of Daniel that the distinctive name of Israel's God, Yhwh / the Lord, is not used, except a few times in chapter 9. Yet there is no doubt that the God of Daniel is indeed the Lord. The extensive presence of fire is perhaps the clearest symbolic indication that the royal figure on the throne is the Lord, the God of Israel, for fire is a primary symbol of the Lord's presence in the Old Testament (e.g., at Mount Sinai/Horeb, Exod. 3:2; 19:18; Deut. 4:12; and in relation to Elijah and Elisha, 2 Kings 2:11; 6:17).

In those infrequent places where the Old Testament imaginatively depicts the Lord in His own realm, it is always by analogy with an earthly king surrounded by courtiers (Job 1:6–12; 2:1–6; 1 Kings 22:19–23). So too in Daniel 7, though the divine court is seen to be specifically a law court, a place of justice.

> I watched then because of the noise of the arrogant words that the horn was speaking. And as I watched, the beast was put to death, and its body destroyed and given over to be burned with fire. As for the rest of the beasts, their dominion was taken

away, but their lives were prolonged for a season and a time.
(Dan. 7:11–12)

The text reverts to prose to tell what happens. It is not quite
clear how the vision of the beasts and the vision of the court
interact, but presumably the beasts are in some way brought
before the figure on the throne. An initial focus is the horn with
its arrogant words, which Daniel continues to hear even as he
also sees the vision of God. Yet almost as soon as the visions
of the beast and of the court are juxtaposed, the fourth beast
with all its horns is destroyed. Although the other beasts remain
alive, they survive only in diminished mode. The judgment of
God overcomes the beasts. Yet then there is a new development,
a new image, whose telling becomes poetic again:

> As I watched in the night visions,
>
>> I saw one like a human being [Aramaic "one like a son
>>> of man"]
>> coming with the clouds of heaven.
>> And he came to the Ancient One [Aramaic "the An-
>>> cient of Days"]
>> and was presented before him.
>> To him was given dominion [*sholtān*]
>> and glory and kingship,
>> that all peoples, nations, and languages
>> should serve him.
>> His dominion is an everlasting dominion [*sholtān
>>> 'ālam*]
>> that shall not pass away,
>> and his kingship is one
>> that shall never be destroyed. (Dan. 7:13–14)

This human-looking figure in some way clearly displaces the
beasts through the will of the divine figure on the throne. The

imagery suggests that the Ancient One on the throne highly honors this human-looking figure.

> The clouds of heaven are a common poetic symbol of divine presence and motion—for example, "You [LORD] make the clouds your chariot" (Ps. 104:3), "See, the LORD is riding on a swift cloud and comes to Egypt" (Isa. 19:1). If the human figure "comes with the clouds," this is a mark of divine honor, rather like the chariot and horses of fire that accompanied Elijah's being taken up to heaven (2 Kings 2:11).

Dominion that was previously exercised by the beasts is now to be exercised by this human-looking figure, and this dominion, unlike that of the beasts, is without limit both in extent ("all peoples") and in time ("shall never be destroyed"). The transfer is complete, and the difference is fundamental.

> As for me, Daniel, my spirit was troubled within me, and the visions of my head terrified me. I approached one of the attendants to ask him the truth concerning all this. So he said that he would disclose to me the interpretation of the matter: "As for these four great beasts, four kings shall arise out of the earth. But the holy ones of the Most High shall receive the kingdom and possess the kingdom forever ['ad 'ālmā']—forever and ever." (Dan. 7:15–18)

Daniel remains both fearful and apparently uncomprehending. But since, in his dream, he is clearly located somewhere in or close to the divine court of justice, he is able to approach one of the courtiers, presumably an angelic being, and ask for the meaning of what he is seeing. The identity of the figure on the throne is clearly not in question, so the answer relates solely to the other key figures. The beasts are human kings, presumably representing also their kingdoms. The "one like a human being" who receives the everlasting dominion represents "the holy ones of the Most High"—which in the wider narrative world of the

book of Daniel would most naturally be those Jewish people
who are struggling to remain faithful in exile.

> Although there is little doubt that the intended referent of the vision at this
> point is faithful Jews of the 160s↓, I am passing over a complex subquestion
> about whether the human-looking figure may in the first instance be an
> angel such as Michael who, together with other angels, plays a significant
> role in the latter part of the book (Dan. 10:13, 20–21; 12:1), and whether
> the "holy ones" may also be angelic figures (in keeping with common He-
> brew/Aramaic idiom). Since Daniel 7:27 is explicit that "*the people* of the
> holy ones of the Most High" will receive an everlasting dominion, and since
> Michael represents and seems to act in synergy with the Jewish people, a
> possible angelic referent would make no real difference to the substantive
> meaning of the vision for its Jewish recipients.

At this point the narration of the dream might have con-
cluded. But it continues with Daniel asking to know more about
the fourth beast with its various horns, especially the one that
spoke arrogantly (Dan. 7:19–20). Daniel indeed sees more:
"This horn made war with the holy ones and was prevailing
over them, until the Ancient One came; then judgment was given
for the holy ones of the Most High" (7:21–22). But although
a fuller account is then given of the power and violence of the
fourth beast with its war against the holy ones of the Most
High and its attempt "to change the sacred seasons and the law"
(7:23–25), the same outcome is reaffirmed: the dominion of the
fourth beast will be removed, and kingship and dominion will
instead be given to the holy ones of the Most High, and their
kingdom and dominion will be everlasting (7:26–27). Only then
does the account end, and Daniel is left to ponder it (7:28).

The Book of Daniel in the Context of the Maccabean Revolt

As with *Aeneid* 1, one of the first questions to ask, as we
turn to "the world behind the text" (the context of composition

and initial use), concerns identity—in Daniel 7, the identity of the beasts and the holy ones. For although the identification of the beasts as kings, and of the human figure as the holy ones, would presumably have been sufficient for the initial recipients of the book to know who was meant, the passing of time can make the context of origin obscure and also change readers' perspectives. However, the determining of these identities is inseparable from determining the context of the book's initial appearance and use.

The strong scholarly consensus is that although the book tells of the figure of Daniel in Babylon in the sixth century↓, and although Daniel speaks extensively in the first person, there is nonetheless an important difference between the world within the text and the world behind the text. There has indeed been a long tradition among both Jews and Christians of effectively equating these two worlds, straightforwardly inferring the nature of the world behind the text from the content of the world within the text—that is, the Daniel who speaks in chapters 7–12 is an exiled Jew of the sixth century↓ who speaks of the distant future and who is in some way responsible for the content of the book as a whole. The modern consensus, however, is that there are very good reasons to reckon that the world behind the text is not the sixth century but the second century↓, specifically the time of Jewish resistance to Antiochus Epiphanes in the 160s↓.[21]

21. The old accounts by S. R. Driver of the reasons for adopting this view remain exceptionally clear and helpful, even if some of the details have been modified in subsequent scholarship. See his *Daniel*, CBSC (Cambridge: Cambridge University Press, 1905), ix–xcviii, 94–102, or, more briefly, his *Introduction to the Literature of the Old Testament*, ITC (Edinburgh: T&T Clark, 1897), 488–515. For a more recent discussion of issues related to Daniel's composition and interpretation, see, e.g., John J. Collins, *Daniel*, Hermeneia (Minneapolis: Fortress, 1993); John Goldingay, *Daniel*, WBC 30 (Dallas: Word, 1989); or Carol A. Newsom (with Brennan W. Breed), *Daniel*, OTL (Louisville: Westminster John Knox, 2014). I shall pass over numerous technical issues having to do with the formation and interpretation of the book of Daniel in general, and of Dan. 7 in particular, as they do not really make a difference to my main argument.

The Jewish nation lost its independence after its defeat by the Babylonians in the sixth century↓. When power passed from Babylon to Persia, and then from Persia to Alexander the Great and his commanders, so too did dominion over the Jewish nation in its historic home in and around Jerusalem. Of particular interest to the Jewish people were two of Alexander's commanders who established their dominions as the Jews' immediate neighbors: Seleucus and the Seleucid kings to the north in Syria, and Ptolemy and the Ptolemaic dynasty to the south and west in Egypt. Control of the Jewish territory, which lay between these two realms, was regularly disputed by the Seleucids and the Ptolemies (disputes refracted in Dan. 11 in terms of the king of the north and the king of the south).

One key figure was the Seleucid king Antiochus IV, who ruled from 175 to 164↓. This Antiochus was known as "Epiphanes," a divine epithet of a kind not uncommon in Hellenistic culture (Epiphanes is an abbreviation of *Theos Epiphanēs*, "a god who manifests/reveals himself"). Although sources for the period are limited, and our knowledge is rather fragmentary, Antiochus apparently attempted to impose Greek culture on the Jews and thereby, at least from a traditional Jewish perspective, fundamentally change Jewish identity and a Jewish outlook on the world—something not attempted by either the Babylonians or the Persians.[22] It appears that Antiochus's aggression against the Jews in Judea is the original historical setting for Daniel 7 and for the book of Daniel as a whole (even if earlier material may be incorporated). The fourth and final beast, which is clearly the primary antagonist within the vision, is the Hellenistic empire founded by Alexander the Great and divided among his commanders after his death. The fourth beast's aggressive little horn with human-like eyes and arrogant speech is Antiochus Epiphanes. The holy ones

22. A primary narrative source is 1 Maccabees 1:20–64.

of the Most High, symbolically represented by the human-like figure who comes to the divine throne, are those Jews who are resisting Antiochus.

At the symbolic heart of Antiochus's attempted hellenization was a move forcibly to abolish Jewish worship in the Jerusalem temple and to replace it with Greek rituals and practices. This assault is succinctly refracted in the latter part of Daniel's vision:

> He [the little horn of the fourth beast] shall speak
>> words against the Most High,
>> shall wear out the holy ones of the Most High,
>> and shall attempt to change the sacred seasons and
>> the law;
> and they shall be given into his power
>> for a time, two times, and half a time. (Dan. 7:25)

The reaction that this provoked, the Maccabean Revolt, led to Jewish military victory over the Seleucids, the rededication of the Jerusalem temple, and a period of Jewish independence from Seleucid (and Ptolemaic) dominion. This too is refracted, though presumably still in anticipation, in the latter part of Daniel's vision:

> Then the court shall sit in judgment,
>> and his dominion shall be taken away,
>> to be consumed and totally destroyed.
> The kingship and dominion
>> and the greatness of the kingdoms under the whole
>> heaven
>> shall be given to the people of the holy ones of the
>> Most High;
> their kingdom shall be an everlasting kingdom,
>> and all dominions shall serve and obey them. (Dan.
>> 7:26–27)

The holy ones, who in the world of the text appear to be the Jews of an unspecified place and time, are, in the world behind the text, the Jews of Judea who are resisting Antiochus.

> Despite the scholarly consensus about the identity of the fourth beast and its little horn, the identification of the four beasts/kingdoms overall is not in fact entirely straightforward. Even if the identity of the fourth beast as the Hellenistic empire would have been clear to the initial recipients of the book of Daniel, the question of whether all readers/hearers would have been expected to recognize the first three kings and empires as those of Babylonia, Media, and Persia is perhaps a moot point. Israel's traditions generally (other than those in the book of Daniel) draw attention to only three nations that dominated Israel—Assyria, Babylon, and Persia. So how does one go from these three to four, with Greece as the final beast?
>
> An important interpretive role is played by Daniel 2, where Nebuchadnezzar has a dream whose meaning is given to him by Daniel. The dream is of a statue made up of four parts, each of which is made of a distinct element: gold, silver, bronze, and a mixture of iron and clay. These are said to be four kingdoms that succeed one another, and the first of them is explicitly Nebuchadnezzar and his Babylonian kingdom. Eventually a stone destroys the statue and replaces it with a mountain that represents a kingdom set up by God to endure forever (2:31–45). The analogy with the vision of Daniel 7—four human powers that pass away, one divinely given power that endures—is clear. It means that the first beast in Daniel 7 is also Babylon (and so the earlier dominion of Assyria is ruled out). Nonetheless, the identification of the two middle beasts as Media and Persia, prior to the coming of Greece, may not have been obvious to any but the *cognoscenti*, though Medes and Persians are clearly intended because of their mention elsewhere within Daniel (e.g., 5:28–31 [Aramaic 6:1]; 8:20–21).

The general reckoning that the book of Daniel is originally a form of resistance literature makes it likely that one can determine the time of the composition of Daniel's vision with some precision. The Jews had already experienced Antiochus's aggression—hence the prominence of the arrogant horn and its aggressive actions within the vision. But they had not yet experienced deliverance from Antiochus—hence the vision of the destruction of the fourth beast with its horn and the transferal of dominion to the holy ones instead. If the purpose of resistance literature is to strengthen the faithful in their fight to remain faithful, then it is most likely to be produced when the struggle is going on, rather than before the struggle begins or after it finishes. Insofar as we can date Antiochus's assault and the Maccabean resistance between 167 and 164↓, some specific time within that period must be the original context of the vision of Daniel 7.

Conclusion

So far, I have tried to read the world within the text of both *Aeneid* 1 and Daniel 7 with full imaginative seriousness, and the imaginative mode has been primarily historical, trying to depict the meaning of these texts in themselves as writings of antiquity. Relatedly, I have given an account of the world behind the text in historical-critical mode, a mode which recognizes that the formative context behind the text may be distant in both space and time from the world depicted in the text itself.

One preliminary point for comparative reflection on *Aeneid* 1 and Daniel 7 relates to the nature of the religious vision in each. For both Virgil and his audience, the depiction of the gods in Homeric mode was a cultural idiom that most likely would not have been taken "literally"; Romans would not have confused the divine powers in which they believed with Virgil's imaginative portrayal in a time-honored mode warranted by the huge cultural prestige of Homer. Jupiter had a major temple in Rome, which had been restored by Augustus; but that did not mean that Jupiter was necessarily thought about in the modes of epic poetry. Virgil's own views, insofar as these can be discerned from his writings,[23] appear to have elements of

23. W. A. Camps offers a helpful framing of the issues in *An Introduction to Virgil's* Aeneid (Oxford: Oxford University Press, 1969), 41–50. Also useful is Susanna Morton Braund's "Virgil and the Cosmos: Religious and Philosophical Ideas," in *The*

both the Stoic and the Epicurean outlook, with a predominance of the Stoic in the *Aeneid*. The weight of the religious outlook in the *Aeneid* lies not in the person of Jupiter but rather in the notion of fate (*fatum*) and in the way Aeneas conducts himself as dutiful/respectful (*pius*—a term whose rich resonances in ancient Roman culture are hard to capture concisely in English). It may be, however, that part of Jupiter's importance lies in the extent to which he can be conceived of as a personification of fate. The overall vision of the poem contains a certain sense of fate that becomes providential destiny for Rome, with the corollary for Aeneas that he must endure faithfully to realize a greater goal.

There are both similarities and differences between *Aeneid* 1 and Daniel 7. Old Testament writers generally are happy to imagine and depict their deity in certain familiar human categories—that is, anthropomorphically, in Daniel 7 in terms of a royal judge in a court—and in that sense there is some comparability with Virgil's anthropomorphic depiction of the gods. Likewise, those Jews producing and receiving Daniel 7 would most likely not have taken its scenario "literally" any more than Virgil and his audience would have done with Jupiter and Venus. But this is not to deny that in each context the literary scenario would be taken seriously in terms of its content. The qualities of faithfulness and endurance that are envisaged for the Jewish recipients of the Ancient One's bequest are not the same as, but are certainly comparable to, the faithful endurance that Aeneas must display.

However, the figure of God, the Ancient One, plays a role for the Jewish writers that Jupiter does not play for the Romans. For the LORD is the focus of Israel's devotion and loyalty, and the fundamental constituent of their identity—as perhaps most

Cambridge Companion to Virgil, ed. Charles Martindale (Cambridge: Cambridge University Press, 1997), 204–21.

famously expressed in the Shema (Deut. 6:4–9). Within the book of Daniel this allegiance is seen in the unswerving and life-defining adherence to the God of Israel that is displayed by Shadrach, Meshach, and Abednego (Dan. 3) as well as by Daniel himself (Dan. 6). Also, divine sovereignty is differently nuanced in the *Aeneid* and in Daniel. Jupiter's sovereignty is constrained by fate and interactions with differently minded deities; they are lesser but still significant. In contrast, the Lord has no peers, His sovereignty has no formal constraint, and He overthrows the beasts, which symbolize violence and injustice. However, those beasts are not prevented from existing in the first place, and there is no interest in explaining their presence, apparently because they represent given realities within the world.

There is also a question about the degree to which the dominion given by the Ancient One is in fact envisaged as the same as the dominion given by Jupiter—but that will be considered further in the following chapters.

✳ ✳ ✦ ✳ ✳ ✦ ✳ ✳

On Terminology for Calendar Dates

There is an unresolved problem about how best to refer to calendar dates. The calendar that is now used worldwide originated as a specifically Christian calendar that sees the birth of Jesus Christ as a key turning point in history and so divides history into two periods: the time before Christ, traditionally designated BC (Before Christ), and the time since Christ, traditionally designated AD (Anno Domini ["in the year of the Lord"])—though why the latter designation should be in Latin while the former is in English (rather than the Latin "Ante Christum") has never been clear to me.

This calendar is ascribed to the work of a sixth-century monk, Dionysius Exiguus. There are two intrinsic problems with Dionysius's calendar. One is that his computation of the beginning of the period AD most likely does not in fact exactly correspond to the probable year of Christ's birth, but is off by four or five years. The other problem is that Dionysius did not include a year zero; the mathematical importance of zero was appreciated in a European context only at a later period, through the influence of Arabic mathematical thinking. Nonetheless, this is the calendar now in almost universal use, and no alternative is likely to replace it.

The problem is how best to designate years in a post-Christendom world that is increasingly secularized and religiously plural. Many people are happy to use the traditional terms "BC" and "AD" simply because they are time-honored and culturally recognized and need no more imply religious belief, or acceptance of Jesus as Lord, than does the continued designation and celebration of December 25 as "Christmas"[1] or continued reference to Jesus as "Christ" (just as non-Buddhists are happy to refer to Siddhartha Gautama as "Buddha"). But many scholars in particular have become unhappy with calendar terminology that privileges a Christian frame of reference and so have looked for an alternative.

The most common alternative is BCE (Before the Common Era) and CE (Common Era). Yet the term "common" looks to be something of a polite fiction. For what is "common" about the Common Era, and what previous state of affairs in the ancient world changed to make it "common," if not the birth of Christ? In terms of Western Europe, the best candidate would be the advent of the Roman Empire—but this would hardly be significant for the Chinese. To be sure, Jewish scholars have used the terminology on the basis that the time period CE could be said to be common to both Jews and Christians. This has proved to have some value in the context of Jewish-Christian dialogue. But in relation to any other living tradition of thought and life, the notion of a Common Era makes little sense. Islam, for example, has its own calendar, which begins in the time of Muhammad.

James Turner, in his important book *Philology*, argues for the use of BCE and CE on the grounds that "the adoption of Christian time reckoning as the international standard has

---

1. There was a notorious attempt by the Birmingham, UK, city council in the 1990s to replace "Christmas" with "Winterval" in the city's annual festivities. It failed, apparently because the multiethnic and religiously diverse people of Birmingham did not find "Christmas" as problematic as their secularized councillors thought they should.

made it truly 'common,' no longer distinctively Christian." As a
comment on today's world, that is clearly true. However, if the
turning point between BCE and CE comes not in the modern
world but already in the ancient world, this modern situation
does not resolve the issue of thinking constructively about date
nomenclature in the ancient world, if BC and AD are perceived
as problematic. Turner also observes that there are interesting
historical precedents for "Common Era" from a time prior to
any anxiety about Christian terminology. "It appeared in the
title of the great astronomer Johannes Kepler's *Eclogae chroni-
cae* (1615)," where "the full title promises that Kepler will show
that 'the passion, death, and resurrection of Our Lord Jesus
Christ' occurred in 'anno aerae nostrae vulgaris 31'—that is,
in 'year 31 of our common era.'" Also "the first volume of
Ludovico Muratori's *Annali d'Italia* (1744) began, as its title
page proclaimed, 'Dall'Anno primo dell'Era volgare'—from
the first year of the common era."[2] Yet is this terminological
precedent a conceptual precedent? "Common" here most likely
envisages the universality of Christian faith, as distinct from the
more restricted particularity of its Jewish antecedent, and so
has a distinctively Christian theological coloring, which is the
very thing that "Common Era" today is trying to escape from.

Why discuss this issue here? In terms of my primary concern
with how one should approach the Bible, it is hardly needed.
Nonetheless, insofar as the wider context of my argument is
the need to rethink what is appropriate for Christian faith in
an increasingly post-Christian culture where Christians have
minority status, the terminology for calendar dates poses a nice
puzzle. The familiar calendrical system, somewhat like the Bible,
was formed in a Christian culture and is still used beyond that
culture. So how best should this calendrical system be referred

2. James Turner, *Philology: The Forgotten Origins of the Modern Humanities*
(Princeton and Oxford: Princeton University Press, 2014), xix, 387.

to and thought about, if there is no realistic alternative to its continued use? (The great revolutions of modernity in France and Russia, in the late eighteenth and early twentieth centuries respectively, both tried to fashion a new calendar to indicate the thoroughness of their break with the past and the newness of the era they were heralding. The fact that each revolution was unsuccessful in this regard, despite the energy for change that each unleashed, suggests that no other attempted replacement would be likely to succeed.)

My concern in chapter 2 was to look at how the Bible can legitimately be handled in nonreligious ways. By analogy, there should presumably be good methods of handling a Christianly formed dating system in ways that do not require Christian perspectives. My objection to BCE/CE is not that it is not Christian but that it is—put bluntly—thoroughly misleading, for the reasons just given.

So I conclude this discussion with a suggestion, a thought experiment, which I hope may spark some debate. If there is no real alternative to using a numerical reckoning of years according to Dionysius's calendar, then it makes sense to adopt as an alternative to BC and AD a system that focuses solely on the numbers themselves rather than on their possible implications (whether that be Christ or "common era"). The significant distinction is between the period of time when the reckoning of years decreases (the numbers approach zero) and when it increases (the numbers move away from zero). The former could be, say, "Years Decreasing" (YD), while the latter could comparably be "Years Increasing" (YI). In written form, however, it might be simplest just to use a directional arrow: ↓ or ↑. Thus, Rome was reckoned to be founded in 753↓, while Jerusalem fell to the Romans in 70↑. As a small wave of the flag, I adopt my own proposal in this book so that readers can at least see how it looks in practice.

3

Towards Privileged Perspectives

So far, I have sketched some of the difficulties with the notion that the Bible is "the most valuable thing that this world affords," a value rooted in its containing "the lively oracles of God," which give wisdom for life.

First, there has been a general deprivileging of the Bible in the modern world, on the grounds that it is fundamentally a complex human artifact that is in principle not different in kind from other human artifacts—not a key to understanding God and the world, but essentially a collection of Jewish and Christian viewpoints arising from, and expressive of, an ancient world that has long since passed away, even if this collection has also become a cultural classic through its use in Christian civilizations that have themselves passed away. Second, the human dimensions of the Bible have generally ceased to be seen as in some sense a way to, or transparency for, God. This is not least because what the Bible says about God can be seen in the same way as what other ancient texts also say about their gods. Such material we consider today to be eloquent of the

79

psychology and sociology of the ancients, but not a window onto transcendent and enduring divine reality.

I have also sketched some of the ways in which scholars and general readers can and do still take the Bible seriously, although without the dimension of faith that is the classic Christian stance. But insofar as the Bible is "the most valuable thing that this world affords," it is more than fascinating history to be explored or a cultural classic to be taken seriously, even if it is both of those things as well. What, then, does that "more" involve? How might one articulate an approach that combines taking the Bible seriously with the dimension of faith? This is not to rule out the legitimacy of holding these things apart, but rather to show how they can well be brought together, should one wish to participate in the historic Christian stance towards the Bible.

I want to come at this question via a notable and widespread phenomenon: the fact that people privilege particular things for making sense of life. I will then set an approach to the Bible within this context.

Understanding and Evaluating Life through Particular Lenses

Jonathan Z. Smith on "Canon"

In a fascinating 1977 essay, historian of religion Jonathan Z. Smith asks the question of whether the categories that historians of religion use might be informed by the categories and content of a particular religious tradition, such as Judaism.[1] He takes the issue of "sacred persistence," as focused in the phenomenon of canon, as his case study.

1. Jonathan Z. Smith, "Sacred Persistence: Toward a Redescription of Canon," in *Imagining Religion: From Babylon to Jonestown* (Chicago and London: University of Chicago Press, 1982), 36–52.

Starting with the everyday realities of food and drink, Smith observes that although worldwide there appear to be virtually no limits to what people eat and drink, nonetheless within any given culture what people actually eat and drink may often have marked limits. Yet once a restricted selection is made out of the vast range of possible things to eat and drink, the preparation of what is selected is characterized by great variety. For example, although wine can be made from almost any fruit, flower, or root, most people focus on the grape, and show great breadth and variety in the types of grapes they grow and how they grow them in order to produce wine. *Initial reduction and then ingenious variegation is the pattern*. Smith further observes that "the same sort of process may be observed with respect to every important human phenomenon."[2]

On this basis, he turns to the phenomenon of a canon and its interpretation by the community that maintains it. He holds that

> the radical and arbitrary reduction represented by the notion of canon and the ingenuity represented by the rule-governed exegetical enterprise of applying the canon to every dimension of human life is that most characteristic, persistent, and obsessive religious activity.[3]

Smith is clear that canon and interpretation belong together:

> Where there is a canon, it is possible to predict the *necessary* occurrence of a hermeneute, of an interpreter whose task it is continually to extend the domain of the closed canon over everything that is known or everything that exists *without* altering the canon in the process.[4]

2. Smith, "Sacred Persistence," 40.
3. Smith, "Sacred Persistence," 43.
4. Smith, "Sacred Persistence," 48.

The latter part of the essay displays Smith's informed imagination at work in offering fascinating examples of how this phenomenon of canon—though usually associated with "peoples of the book" and considered to be a "relatively rare phenomenon within the history of religions, even among literate groups"[5]—is in fact characteristic also of nonliterate societies if one recognizes how certain designs, forms, and objects function "canonically" in particular communities through an initial narrowing of focus accompanied by interpretive breadth and ingenuity.

I propose to take Smith's suggestive discussion in a direction of which he himself might not approve, for it is a looser sense of restriction and interpretive amplification that I wish to consider. My concern is with the way in which people generally, at least in contemporary Western culture, tend to interpret basic life issues and the question of God by an initial narrowing of focus and a subsequent expanding of the interpretive power of that narrowed focus (although the complex interpretive activities tend to remain low-level until a stance becomes shared and receives social acceptance and recognition). The general point is that, among the myriad of things that happen in life and are present in the world, people are necessarily selective in choosing which particular things they will give weight to in understanding the world and their position in it. A few things are almost always privileged over all other things; and although the decision about what to privilege is of course revisable, the basic pattern of selecting, privileging, and then interpreting widely on that basis almost always remains.

Charles Darwin's Attitude to Christian Faith

Let me take the example of one of the greatest and most influential of all scientists, Charles Darwin. My concern is not

5. Smith, "Sacred Persistence," 44.

with his science but with his theology and his faith, or rather his famous loss of faith.

Richard Dawkins depicts Darwin's loss of Christian faith thus:

> Charles Darwin lost his [faith] with the help of [a wasp]: "I cannot persuade myself," Darwin wrote, "that a beneficent and omnipotent God would have designedly created the Ichneumonidae with the express intention of their feeding with the living bodies of Caterpillars."[6]

Dawkins of course acknowledges that Darwin's gradual loss of faith had complex causes. Nonetheless, Darwin's appeal to the ichneumon wasp, which Dawkins characterizes as "aphoristic," has subsequently become a standard topos in science and religion debates as paradigmatic of a natural phenomenon that appears to be incompatible with a Christian belief in a beneficent and omnipotent God. Dawkins clarifies:

> The macabre habits to which he [Darwin] referred are shared by their cousins the digger wasps. . . . A female digger wasp not only lays her egg in a caterpillar (or grasshopper or bee) so that her larva can feed on it but . . . she carefully guides her sting into each ganglion of the prey's central nervous system, so as to paralyze it *but not kill it.* This way, the meat keeps fresh. It is not known whether the paralysis acts as a general anaesthetic, or if it is like curare in just freezing the victim's ability to move. If the latter, the prey might be aware of being eaten alive from inside but unable to move a muscle to do anything about it.[7]

6. Richard Dawkins, *River Out of Eden: A Darwinian View of Life* (London: Weidenfeld & Nicholson, 1995), 95. The reference is to an 1860 letter of Darwin to Asa Gray, for which see *The Life and Letters of Charles Darwin, Including an Autobiographical Chapter*, ed. Francis Darwin (London: John Murray, 1887), 2:312. In context, Darwin's point is that such things make it impossible for him to find divine "design" in the world.

7. Dawkins, *River Out of Eden*, 95.

For Dawkins himself, as for not a few others, this particular phenomenon succinctly encapsulates a wider truth about the world we live in:

> If Nature were kind, she would at least make the minor concession of anaesthetizing caterpillars before they are eaten alive from within. But Nature is neither kind nor unkind. She is neither against suffering nor for it. Nature is not interested one way or the other in suffering, unless it affects the survival of DNA. . . .
>
> In a universe of blind physical forces and genetic replication, some people are going to get hurt, other people are going to get lucky, and you won't find any rhyme or reason in it, nor any justice. The universe we observe has precisely the properties we should expect if there is, at bottom, no design, no purpose, no evil and no good, nothing but blind, pitiless indifference. . . .
>
> DNA neither knows nor cares. DNA just is. And we dance to its music.[8]

The ichneumon wasp becomes shorthand for a wide range of natural phenomena, and thereby also becomes a privileged focus for interpreting the world more generally and for showing the hopeless inadequacy of religious belief in relation to natural realities.

To return to Darwin and the likely complexity of factors within his loss of faith: one possible contributory factor, on which many recent biographers have laid emphasis, is the death of Darwin's favorite daughter, Annie, at the age of ten in April 1851. Darwin's major modern biographers, Adrian Desmond and James Moore,[9] drawing on Darwin's notebooks and letters, depict him in 1850–51 as already in the advanced stages of departing from Christian faith (in a particular Victorian form),

8. Dawkins, *River Out of Eden*, 131, 133.
9. Adrian Desmond and James Moore, *Darwin* (London: Michael Joseph, 1991).

on the pattern of Francis Newman (younger brother of John Henry Newman, but very different in outlook), whose books he was reading: "Religiously he [Charles Darwin] had moved on, and, as with Newman, the Bible had disintegrated in his hands—the Old Testament with its Creation legends and moral monstrosities, the New Testament bristling with inconsistencies and myths. . . . Emotional attachment to Christianity was not enough; faith had to comply with reason, morality, and historical evidence. There was no stopping short at Unitarianism. . . . Christianity had to be rejected once and for all." Annie's death, however, taking place just after Easter, was decisive: "There was no straw to clutch, no promised resurrection. Christian faith was futile. . . . Annie's cruel death destroyed Charles's tatters of belief in a moral, just universe. Later he would say that this period chimed the final death-knell for his Christianity, even if it had been a long, drawn-out process of decay. . . . Charles now took his stand as an unbeliever."[10] The caption to a photograph of Annie Darwin that her father cherished after her death includes: "Her tragic death at Easter 1851 destroyed the final shreds of Darwin's Christianity."[11]

Perhaps surprisingly, given the confident, moving, and persuasive picture that Desmond and Moore paint, their account of the role that Annie's death played in Darwin's loss of faith has recently been challenged by John van Wyhe and Mark Pallen,[12] on the grounds that there is no clear evidence to connect Annie's death with Darwin's loss of faith. Indeed, van Wyhe and Pallen contend that such an account, despite being widespread in recent biographers, is "entirely speculative" and is no more than "a modern Darwin myth."[13] They argue that Darwin had already lost his faith at an earlier period, substantially by the end of the 1830s.

10. Desmond and Moore, *Darwin*, 378, 384, 387.
11. Desmond and Moore, *Darwin*, opposite p. 333.
12. John van Wyhe and Mark J. Pallen, "The 'Annie Hypothesis': Did the Death of His Daughter Cause Darwin to 'Give Up Christianity'?" *Centaurus* 54, no. 2 (2012): 105–23.
13. Van Wyhe and Pallen, "'Annie Hypothesis,'" 120, 105.

A nonspecialist such as myself who lacks the necessary familiarity with the primary Darwin documents can hardly adjudicate such a divergence of understanding of the role of Annie's death. I would simply offer two observations. First, in a matter such as loss of faith, not least when Darwin remained close to his wife, Emma, who retained a firm faith, finality of conviction in Darwin's mind and heart may perhaps have been less clear and more intermittent than retrospective interpreters have sometimes supposed. Second, there are questions about what "faith" means in this context. My impression from browsing the literature is that the significant issue is not Darwin's formal adherence to Christian faith (Jesus, Bible, church), which seems to have fallen by the wayside sooner rather than later, but rather the length of time before Darwin finally relinquished his formative theology—that is, his William Paley–influenced acknowledgment of God as the author of design in the universe—as this was something that lingered long before he finally moved from "theist" (still at the time of writing *Origin of Species*, and so subsequent to Annie's death) to "agnostic."[14]

Nonetheless, even if the impact of Annie's death on Darwin's loss of faith remains debatable, I hope that my appeal to this paradigmatic example of a widespread phenomenon—that is, allowing tragedy to lead to abandonment of faith in God—will remain meaningful, even if Darwin may or may not be a good exemplar.

One cannot but feel for any parent who loses a beloved child in the early years of life, and Darwin would by no means be untypical in allowing such a tragedy to finalize his abandonment of Christian faith in God. A particular tragedy is given a privileged position for deciding about God and, by extension, other related issues of faith.

It is important to note, however, that this kind of decision to abandon faith is not really a matter of reason or logic. Annie's death, sadly, was not unusual. If one looks at rates of infant and child mortality throughout history (impossible though it is to be precise), huge numbers of human beings have died at the same or at an earlier age than Annie.

14. There is an illuminating account, in Darwin's own words, of his gradual relinquishing of acknowledgment of the existence of God as First Cause in F. Darwin, *Life and Letters of Charles Darwin*, 1:307–13.

Historical demographics is a challenging discipline that constantly struggles both with the availability of evidence and with questions of its reliability and interpretation. But let me briefly offer two illustrative citations.

Robert Woods has studied the demography of Victorian England—that is, the world of Darwin. In discussing a chart with evidence from the 1580s to the 1940s (which he emphasizes "should be treated with some caution"), he says, "Before the twentieth century the chances of a newly born baby surviving to its fifth birthday were normally less than 75 per cent and, on occasions, closer to 70 per cent or even lower. However the childhood mortality rate was far from constant."[15] This means that some 25 to 30 percent of Annie's contemporaries would have died before they were five years old.

Roger Bagnall and Bruce Frier have studied the demography of ancient Egypt in the early Roman Empire—that is, somewhere close in place and time to the origins of Christian faith. They say of female mortality during this period: "Despite obvious uncertainties, we think it warranted to reconstruct for Roman Egypt female life expectancy at birth from 20 to 25 years, life expectancy at age 10 of from 34.5 to 37.5 years. . . ."[16] These figures are so far removed from the experience of the contemporary Western world that it is easy to forget that modern rates of life expectancy are the exception, rather than the rule, in the history of humankind.

Apart from premature individual deaths for health reasons, major tragedies, both natural and humanly caused, have happened throughout history. If one is older than a small child, one should not be able to believe in God without being aware that tragedies happen. Darwin in his earlier adult life, when he still had some kind of Christian faith, could not but have been aware that tragedies happen. However, it was not tragedies in general but one particular tragedy that appears finally to have made the difference for him. But why, as a matter of theological or philosophical principle—with regard to possible belief in a sovereign and good God—should a single tragedy make the

15. Robert Woods, *The Demography of Victorian England and Wales* (Cambridge: Cambridge University Press, 2000), 251–52.
16. Roger S. Bagnall and Bruce W. Frier, *The Demography of Roman Egypt* (Cambridge: Cambridge University Press, 1994), 90.

difference? Why should *one* tragedy *here* weigh more heavily than *numerous* tragedies *elsewhere*?

Darwin's outlook appears in certain ways to be widely shared.[17] For example, extensive press coverage has been given in recent months and years both to migrants from North Africa and the Middle East who try to cross the Mediterranean and reach Europe, and also to victims of fighting in Syria. No one who follows the news can be unaware of the extensive deaths that have taken place in both contexts. And yet one or two images of children have produced exceptional shock—especially the image of the lifeless body of Aylan Kurdi, who was washed up on a Turkish beach (September 2015). In one sense, such pictures conveyed nothing that people did not already know. Yet these particular pictures somehow communicated a pain and a pathos, and generated an outrage, in a way that more general accounts failed to do.[18]

In all such contexts, it is hard for theological thinking not to be overwhelmed; or, more precisely, it becomes important to see what would count as responsible theological understanding in relation to such tragedies.

Darwin's grasp of theology was markedly different from his grasp of biology. The content of Darwin's faith in his earlier life is articulated by him in his autobiography.[19] When his father proposed that he should become a clergyman—a not uncommon role for a late Georgian gentleman—he asked for time to think about it, and did some reading. He says, "I read with great care *Pearson on the Creed*, and a few other books on divinity; and as I did not then in the least doubt the strict and literal truth of every word

17. The basic point is famously expressed in a cynical quip that is commonly attributed to Stalin: "A single death is a tragedy; a million deaths is a statistic."

18. The pictures of Aylan Kurdi had a real but short-lived impact. A study of donations to the Swedish Red Cross showed that daily contributions increased a hundredfold in the week after Aylan's death. But after five weeks the rate was no different from that of a week before the pictures were taken (Georgie Keate, "How Aylan's Death Really Did Change World's View," *The Times*, January 11, 2017, 9).

19. C. Darwin, "Autobiography," in F. Darwin, *Life and Letters of Charles Darwin*, 1:26–107.

in the Bible, I soon persuaded myself our Creed must be fully accepted."[20] With the benefit of hindsight, it is not difficult to see Darwin's "orthodoxy" as representing an attitude towards the Bible that unsurprisingly led to his rejection of it in due course. Even if an absence of doubt in "the strict and literal truth of every word" in principle represents a positive attitude, it also surely suggests a wooden and unreflective approach to a compilation of ancient sacred texts. Such an unreflective attitude would by no means encourage the exercise of his intellect in any of the subtle, patient, and probing ways in which he exercised it in his biological work. Rather, it would easily encourage an "all or nothing" or "either it's true or it's false" attitude, such that the encountering of problems could more readily lead to wholesale rejection rather than to digging deeper.

Darwin also makes clear that his conceptual frame of reference for understanding God and faith was deeply indebted to the work of William Paley, whose argument from design based on "evidences" initially made good sense to him, as it did to so many of his early nineteenth-century contemporaries: "I was charmed and convinced by the long line of argumentation." Darwin's subsequent rejection of Paley and rejection of faith were related. In the context of telling how he "was very unwilling to give up [his] belief," and yet "disbelief crept over [him] at a very slow rate," he says, "The old argument from design in Nature, as given by Paley, which formerly seemed to me so conclusive, fails, now that the law of natural selection has been discovered."[21]

The significance of Paley's argument from design will be considered again below, in relation to Richard Dawkins.[22] Paley's whole approach has major conceptual deficiencies, and is in fact an aberration in the history of Christian theology. Moreover, even if such an approach might lead to an intellectual acknowledgment of the existence of God, it would hardly entail any sense of trust or personal engagement. Relatedly, if one adopts Paley's "evidences" approach, then the problem of apparently meaningless suffering and death would most likely lead to abstract reflections on how natural processes may or may not relate to divine governance. It would be unlikely to lead to deeper existential engagement with the central symbols and images of Christian faith: Jesus at Gethsemane, Calvary, and the Easter tomb. But when there is tragedy, this is where the Christian imagination should go.

20. C. Darwin, "Autobiography," in F. Darwin, *Life and Letters of Charles Darwin*, 1:45.

21. F. Darwin, *Life and Letters of Charles Darwin*, 1:47, 308–9.

22. See excursus 3.

The basic issue is that humans, although indeed rational creatures, exercise their rationality under the influence of any number of cultural and personal factors. However much we can and should educate and discipline our reason and seek to use it well—indeed, as dispassionately as we are able—countless nonrational factors inevitably affect the actual decisions we make, not least about what to privilege in the way we look at the world. Charles Darwin was no exception.

> Another famous nineteenth-century relinquisher of Christian faith was Friedrich Nietzsche, a writer who remains compelling because of his acuity. Alistair Kee makes clear that for Nietzsche, "atheism . . . was not the outcome of a rational process." Rather, Nietzsche wrote, "he who wants to desert a party or a religion believes it is incumbent upon him to refute it. . . . We did not attach ourself to this party, or religion, on strictly rational grounds: we ought not to affect to have done so when we leave it."[23]

I am suggesting that Darwin's loss of faith (whatever the possibly numerous contributory factors) may be seen as focused in two different natural phenomena: the personal affliction of his daughter's death, and his intellectual puzzlement over the ichneumon wasp—neither of which could he reconcile with faith in a sovereign and good God as portrayed in the Bible and interpreted by the theology of his time. I also want to suggest that in this he can be seen as typical of many people, who will have their own equivalent of personal affliction and/or the puzzle of the ichneumon wasp as their reason for not believing in God. My concern is with the pattern of thought and decision making. There is an initial decision (perhaps sometimes not even consciously made) to select and privilege certain limited phenomena as a focus, and then there is a subsequent utilizing of these privileged phenomena to evaluate issues of belief and the nature of the world in relation to God accordingly.

23. Alistair Kee, *Nietzsche against the Crucified* (London: SCM, 1999), 13. Kee cites Nietzsche's *Human, All Too Human*, 330 (with no further publication information).

If a decision is made "against" God, then joy at new birth, wonder at astonishing natural beauty, revulsion against evil, or amazement at human compassion may still happen, but such things would no longer be indicative of any reality other than that which has been decided upon already.

In this light, I want to return to Jonathan Z. Smith's concern noted above, the phenomenon of canon, and consider the role of the Bible in belief. For one of the things that character-izes a Christian believer is a privileging of the Bible (albeit often selectively) for understanding God and the nature of the world. *Here* we can learn what we most need to know about God and life and death. *Here* basic questions such as "How should we understand the world and our place in it?," "What can I know?," "What should I do?," and "What may I hope?" receive guidance and answers. This is because the Bible offers an overall vision of the world, and of the role of humanity in the world, in the light of God. The world is God's world, to which He gives the gift of life. God unceasingly engages with His world, especially in His initiative in the call of Israel, an initiative that climaxes with the coming of Jesus Christ. Jesus is understood, in classic creedal formulations, to be definitive and unsurpassable both for understanding the reality and na-ture of God and for understanding the nature and purpose of human life. Put differently: Jesus is the one who supremely "makes sense," both in himself and in relation to the puzzling world in which we live. This "making sense" is not a matter of "explaining" things like evil, hatred, cruelty, and suffering, which remain mysterious even as Jesus himself enters into and undergoes them in the fulfillment of his vocation. Indeed, the fact that salvation comes through Jesus being cruelly put to death in the prime of life is the nonnegotiable challenge to all human perspectives that too confidently stipulate what God "ought" to do, or to have done, to deal with the problems of the world. Rather, this "making sense" has to do with setting everything within the context of trust in God and in His good purposes for both time and eternity, which can enable people to face whatever life brings with faith and hope and love. The Bible is privileged because Jesus is privileged, and vice versa. Jesus represents the privileged focus in a believer's vision because of the confidence that in and through Jesus, especially as framed and interpreted by the whole biblical canon, what matters most in life can be rightly understood.

My argument, therefore, is that a Christian privileging of the Bible and of Jesus for understanding God and the world is not in principle different from the privileging of *something* for understanding God and the world that people in general practice. It is not so much that some have a privileged focus and others do not (though there are of course endless variations of approach and emphasis), than that Christians choose to focus *differently* from others, on a particular person and on a particular book that they believe to be a *better* focus than any other: *Look here rather than there.*[24] With any chosen focus, some aspects of life will no doubt remain less able to be made sense of than others, so one corollary of having a privileged focus is deciding which unresolved difficulties one remains happy to live with, difficulties that are recognized but that accompany and do not threaten the chosen privileged focus (other than at times of conversion to a new overall stance).

The Importance of Plausibility Structures

Plausibility Structures 1: The Social Nature of Knowledge

How, then, might people come to see the Christian privileging of Jesus and the Bible as a serious option that they might

24. The basic issue here is perhaps best known today through its articulation in a rather different context "a long time ago in a galaxy far, far away." In *Star Wars: Episode 1—The Phantom Menace*, Qui-Gon Jinn says to the young Anakin, "Always remember: your focus determines your reality."

themselves embrace?[25] Or on what grounds might someone respond positively to the biblical story in such a way as to seek to become part of it as it continues today? I would like to consider these questions via the concept of a plausibility structure, which is the idea that the social and cultural contexts within which people live regularly make a difference to the understandings of life that they hold to be true; among other things, to be surrounded by a consensus can encourage people to adopt that consensus for themselves.

This concept, developed especially in sociology by Peter Berger (among others), and interestingly related to Alasdair MacIntyre's conceptual and historical work on the nature of knowledge and ethics,[26] is in essence simple and straightforward, serving in a contemporary context to resist at least two common problems: individualism and rationalism. The notion of plausibility structures resists individualism by reminding us that individual identity and behavior are always and necessarily bound up with personal relationships and social interactions in a particular historical context. And it resists rationalism by reminding us that individual understanding is bound up with education, socialization, and the use of language in particular historical contexts. No doubt some of these factors can sometimes be so taken for granted, and can feel so natural (as natural as the air one breathes), that people do not appreciate their impact and may even deny it. Nonetheless, the pluralism of contemporary culture should contribute to renewed appreciation of the issues at stake.

Peter Berger and Thomas Luckmann, for example, discuss what is necessary for someone to change their basic perception

25. In this and the following sections I am drawing on my essay "Theological Interpretation, Presuppositions, and the Role of the Church: Bultmann and Augustine Revisited," *Journal of Theological Interpretation* 6, no. 1 (2012): 1–22.

26. See especially his *Whose Justice? Which Rationality?* (London: Duckworth, 1988) and *Three Rival Versions of Moral Enquiry* (London: Duckworth, 1990).

of the world, and with it their identity and allegiance, as in religious conversion:

> The most important social condition is the availability of an effective plausibility structure, that is, a social base serving as the "laboratory" of transformation. This plausibility structure will be mediated to the individual by means of significant others, with whom he must establish strongly affective identification. No radical transformation of subjective reality (including, of course, identity) is possible without such identification, which inevitably replicates childhood experiences of emotional dependency on significant others. These significant others are the guides into the new reality.[27]

"Significant others"—parents, teachers, the friends one makes, the people whose life and speaking or writing one respects and admires, certain public/media personalities—are those who enable one to see that a particular way of living and thinking may be a realistic option. Such "significant others" may, of course, provide plausibility structures for unfaith as much as for faith. Richard Dawkins's writings, and those of the "New Atheists" more generally—not to mention the organizations included in the "list of friendly addresses, for individuals needing support in escaping from religion," which Dawkins considerately provides at the end of *The God Delusion*[28]—comparably contribute to the plausibility structure of living as an atheist.

Significant others not only guide one towards entering a new reality but also play a key role in keeping one there. As Berger and Luckmann put it:

> Conversion may antedate affiliation with the community— Saul of Tarsus sought out the Christian community *after* his

27. Peter L. Berger and Thomas Luckmann, *The Social Construction of Reality: A Treatise in the Sociology of Knowledge* (New York: Doubleday, 1967), 157.
28. Dawkins, *God Delusion*, 375–79.

"Damascus experience." But this is not the point. To have a conversion experience is nothing much. The real thing is to be able to keep on taking it seriously; to retain a sense of its plausibility. *This* is where the religious community comes in. It provides the indispensable plausibility structure for the new reality. In other words, Saul may have become Paul in the aloneness of religious ecstasy, but he could *remain* Paul only in the context of the Christian community that recognized him as such and confirmed the "new being" in which he now located this identity.[29]

Some of the rhetoric here—not only about a conversion experience as "nothing much," but also and especially about Paul's conversion as illustrative of "the aloneness of religious ecstasy"—is conceptually problematic and potentially misleading. But the substantive point about the retentive significance of a plausibility structure is clear and important.

Plausibility Structures 2: Augustine and the Church

The sociological notion of a plausibility structure gives contemporary articulation to a recognition that, in one form or another, is much older. In particular I would like to consider the insights of Augustine (354–430), especially his well-known declaration: "In fact I would not believe the gospel if the authority of the Catholic Church did not move me" (*Ego vero evangelio non crederem nisi me catholicae ecclesiae commoveret auctoritas*).[30] Although this sentence has become a freestanding aphorism, it is easily misunderstood. For this reason it needs briefly to be set in its original context because there is a significant history, especially in Protestant and Enlightenment contexts, of misreading Augustine's words as epitomizing a surrender of intellectual integrity to the say-so of other people who happen to be in positions of institutional authority—thus

29. Berger and Luckmann, *Social Construction of Reality*, 158.
30. Augustine, *Answer to the Letter of Mani Known as* "The Foundation" 5.6.

representing the exact and dismal opposite of Immanuel Kant's famous dictum, *aude sapere*, which might perhaps be rendered "Have the courage to think for yourself."

The sentence comes from one of Augustine's numerous writings against the Manicheans (to whom he himself had once belonged), specifically his *Answer to the Letter of Mani Known as "The Foundation."*[31] His concern is to rebut Manichean claims, and in the process of doing so he discusses basic issues about the nature of faith and how people come to have it.

Augustine sets the context by recognizing how difficult it is to attain authentic faith in God ("Let those rage against you who do not know the labor by which the truth is found and how difficult it is to avoid errors"), and how difficult it was for him personally to do so ("I made myself subject very slowly to the most merciful physician who called me and coddled me in order to wipe away the fog of my mind"). Because of this difficulty Augustine does not wish to talk down to his addressees, simply assuming that he is right and they are wrong, but rather wishes to probe certain key issues as fairly as possible: "Let neither of us say that he has found the truth. Let us seek it in such a way as if neither of us knows it."[32]

How, then, should the argument proceed? Augustine's first move is to resist an intellectualizing of faith (intellectual though he himself is), for that would make true faith the preserve of a select few. He recognizes that a majority within the Catholic Church "are, of course, made completely secure not by the liveliness of their understanding but by the simplicity of their belief." If, then, for the sake of argument, Augustine is not to appeal to what he believes to be truth but which is rejected by the Manicheans, what account can he give of his belonging to

31. I use the translation of Roland Teske, SJ, *The Manichean Debate*, ed. Boniface Ramsey, The Works of Saint Augustine I/19 (Hyde Park, NY: New City Press, 2006), 227–67.

32. Augustine, *Answer to the Letter of Mani* 2.2; 3.3, 4 (Teske, 234–35).

the Catholic Church? He says that, quite apart from true be-lief/wisdom, "there are many other things that most rightfully hold me in her bosom." He then enumerates some key factors:

> The agreement of peoples and nations holds me. The authority begun with miracles, nourished with hope, increased with love, and strengthened with age holds me in the Catholic Church. The succession of priests from the very see of the apostle Peter, to whom after his resurrection the Lord entrusted the feeding of his sheep. . . . Finally, the name "Catholic" holds me in the Catholic Church.[33]

Initially he appeals to catholicity and widespread consensus ("the agreement of peoples and nations"). He then appeals to what is presumably in the first instance the ministry and resurrection of Jesus ("the authority begun with miracles"), but sees its continuation over time in the life of the church ("hope . . . love . . . strengthened with age"). This constitutes an authority that is neither authoritarian nor institutional but is a moral and spiritual reality that has been confirmed repeatedly by lives within the church that have displayed the qualities of hope and love, often in the context of martyrs facing death. Then there is a living continuity of ministry from the very beginnings of the church ("succession of priests . . . sheep"), and there is also the very term "Catholic," presumably because it indicates the universality of what is at stake in belonging to the church. These and other things "hold a believer in the Catholic Church, even if, on account of the slowness of our intelligence or the merit of our life, the truth does not yet reveal itself in full clarity." Augustine thereby offers an account of belonging to the Catholic Church in which intellectual grasp of the truths of the faith is only one factor among others.

It is in this context, when he then goes on to speak of what might move someone to accept the specific content of Christian

---

33. Augustine, *Answer to the Letter of Mani* 4.5 (Teske, 236).

faith when that content is contested (as by Mani and the Manicheans), that Augustine writes his famous words: "In fact I
would not believe the gospel if the authority of the Catholic
Church did not move me." His point has to do not with blind
submission to ecclesial diktat, but rather with the way in which
the faith and life of others persuades him that he too should
enter into and sustain this faith and life, and believe and do
what they believe and do.

The specific issue that Augustine discusses in this context is whether the
gospel can be used to defend the claimed role and authority of Mani. Augustine points out that his reason for believing the gospel is in fact the other
side of the coin of not believing in Mani. His argument, which has a logic
that is both formal and existential, merits a lengthy citation:

> You are perhaps going to read the gospel to me and try to defend
> the person of Mani from there [Augustine cites, as an example,
> reference to the promised Paraclete in John 16:7]. If, then, you
> have found someone who does not yet believe the gospel, what
> would you say to him if he said to you, "I do not believe"? In fact
> I would not believe the gospel if the authority of the Catholic
> Church did not move me. Why should I not believe the people
> whom I obeyed when they told me, "Believe the gospel," when
> they now tell me, "Do not believe the Manicheans"? Choose which
> you want. If you say, "Believe the Catholics," they warn me not
> to place any faith in you. Hence, while believing them, I cannot
> do anything but not believe you. If you say, "Do not believe the
> Catholics," you will not succeed in forcing me into the Manichean
> faith by means of the gospel, since I believed the gospel because
> the Catholics preached it. But if you say, "You were correct to
> believe the Catholics when they praised the gospel, but you were
> not correct to believe them when they disparaged Mani," do you
> think that I am so foolish as to believe what you want me to believe
> and not to believe what you do not want me to believe without
> your having given me any reason? I act much more justly and cau-
> tiously if, because I have already believed the Catholics, I do not
> cross over to you unless you do not order me to believe but make
> me know something with complete clarity and evidence. Hence,
> if you are going to give me a reason, leave the gospel aside. If you
> stick with the gospel, I will stick with those whom I believed when

they taught me the gospel, and at their orders I will absolutely not believe you. If, however, you can perhaps find something perfectly clear in the gospel about the apostleship of Mani, you will weaken for me the authority of the Catholics who command me not to believe you. But if that authority is weakened, I shall not be able to believe the gospel either, since I believed it because of the Catholics. Thus, whatever you produce from the gospel will accomplish nothing with me.[34]

I suggest that Augustine's thought in this whole argument very well represents an ancient formulation of major aspects of the contemporary sociological notion of a plausibility structure.

Plausibility Structures 3: Lesslie Newbigin and the Contemporary Church

The significance of plausibility structures, and especially of the church as a plausibility structure for Christian believing, has increasingly been recognized in recent years and has begun to feature in Christian apologetics.[35] One of its most eloquent and influential exponents has been Lesslie Newbigin, especially in *The Gospel in a Pluralist Society*. Among other things, Newbigin says:

It is essential to recognize that all human thinking takes place within a "plausibility structure" which determines what beliefs are reasonable and what are not. The reigning plausibility structure can only be effectively challenged by people who are fully integrated inhabitants of another. Every person living in a "modern" society is subject to an almost continuous bombardment of ideas, images, slogans, and stories which presuppose a plausibility structure radically different from that which is

---

34. Augustine, *Answer to the Letter of Mani* 5.6 (Teske, 236–37).
35. See, e.g., Dennis Hollinger, "The Church as Apologetic: A Sociology of Knowledge Perspective," in *Christian Apologetics in the Postmodern World*, ed. Timothy R. Phillips and Dennis L. Okholm (Downers Grove, IL: InterVarsity, 1995), 182–93.

controlled by the Christian understanding of human nature and destiny. The power of contemporary media to shape thought and imagination is very great. Even the most alert critical powers are easily overwhelmed.[36]

How, then, can the very heart of the Christian Bible—its portrayal of God and humanity as definitively known in Jesus—be something that is not just a matter for consenting adults in private but a matter of public, indeed ultimate, truth? Newbigin appeals to the importance of particular gatherings of men and women, local congregations, as those contexts that, when functioning properly, enable a biblical perspective on life to become meaningful:

> How is it possible that the gospel should be credible, that people should come to believe that the power which has the last word in human affairs is represented by a man hanging on a cross? I am suggesting that the only answer, the only hermeneutic of the gospel, is a congregation of men and women who believe it and live by it.[37]

Such a context also enables appropriate resistance to other worldviews:

> A Christian congregation is a community in which, through the constant remembering and rehearsing of the true story of human nature and destiny [i.e., constant engagement with Scripture through reading and preaching, and Scripture's incorporation in liturgy and music], an attitude of healthy scepticism can be sustained, a scepticism which enables one to take part in the life of society without being bemused and deluded by its own beliefs about itself.[38]

36. Newbigin, *The Gospel in a Pluralist Society* (London: SPCK, 1989), 228–29.
37. Newbigin, *Gospel in a Pluralist Society*, 227.
38. Newbigin, *Gospel in a Pluralist Society*, 229.

Various questions may no doubt be put to Newbigin's contention that congregations are the primary Christian plausibility structure. For there are many formal and informal, institutional and para-institutional, contexts in which the church is encountered. However, it is probably uncontroversial to say that for most people the primary Christian plausibility structures are local forms and manifestations of Christian community, whether or not those are formal "congregations." Other forms might include, for example, local food banks, street pastors, debt counselors, and Christian groups on a college campus—or even seeing a Billy Graham or Pope Francis on television.

The nature of Newbigin's thesis can perhaps be concisely expressed by modifying a summary statement by Peter Berger: "Any particular religious world will present itself to consciousness as reality only to the extent that its appropriate plausibility structure is kept in existence."[39] I would like to modify this to: *The biblical portrayal of human nature and destiny will present itself to consciousness as reality only to the extent that its appropriate plausibility structure, the Christian church in its many forms, is kept in existence.* This expresses an understanding found both in the Bible and in Jewish and Christian tradition: that the way of living and thinking of particular people who are called to be the people of God—Israel in the Old Testament, the church in the New Testament—is indispensable for giving content to, and making accessible, the enduring and universal significance of the biblical witness (however disappointing and frustrating their performance often is).

The disappointing witness of many Christians is undoubtedly a major obstacle to Christian faith for countless people. Enormous damage has been done in recent years by clergy involved in pedophile practices. Clergy hold recognized and authoritative roles within churches and are called to

39. Peter Berger, *The Social Reality of Religion* (London: Faber & Faber, 1969), 149.

instantiate core values of Christian faith. Thus, to be trustworthy is in principle central to their identity, whatever their intellectual or practical limitations. Children are vulnerable and learn trust from trustworthy people.
When those who especially ought to be trustworthy abuse that trust, the
damage goes deep.

One of the conclusions that follows from all this is that one
can reenvisage the relationship and respective roles of Bible
and church. There is a long and wearying history, since the
sixteenth century, of Christians polarizing Bible and church,
pitting the one over against the other and arguing about which
stands over the other. An understanding that is truer to Christian reality is the complementary nature of Bible and church
(as in the development of the biblical canon in the first place).
The Bible is likely to be recognized as the privileged witness
to God and the world only insofar as living Christian witness
attests at least somewhat persuasively to the truth of biblical
content. The role of significant others and plausibility structures indicates the importance of *trust* and *forming relationships* with other people as the corollary of coming to a point
where one may begin to believe the content of the Bible and to
believe in God through Jesus. The way in which these significant
others live also *interprets* the Bible (for better and for worse)
and thereby gives some sense of what a biblically informed
life may look like.

Plausibility Structures 4: The Privileging of Selected Writings as Scripture

In addition to this general thesis about the interrelated nature of church and Bible, one factor that needs highlighting in
this context is the decision to privilege certain documents as
scriptural—authoritative, canonical, normative—in the first
place. Why should certain ancient documents be recognized
as constituting a Bible at all?

The recognition of certain documents as belonging to a bounded and privileged collection is one of the things that can easily be taken for granted, given the willingness of publishers to go along with this Christian convention. Yet canonical boundaries are routinely set aside as irrelevant by ancient historians; and canonical demarcation is open to question in a contemporary context: Why privilege these writings over others? And if there is a privileged collection, who decides which writings should be included, and on what basis? Why, for example, should the Gospel of John be included, while the Gospel of Thomas is excluded? Why should Israel's wisdom be included, but Egypt's excluded, even if some of Israel's wisdom was influenced by Egyptian wisdom?[40] Such questions about the warrant for a canonical collection have unsurprisingly received increasing attention in recent years.

I presume that publishers (other than explicitly Christian publishing houses) are happy to go along with the Christian canon because, to put it crudely, doing so makes books more likely to sell. Words like "Bible," "Old Testament," and "New Testament" have resonance and recognition and an identifiable, and still significant, market. So even though ancient historians generally ignore canonical distinctions, collections of ancient historical documents are regularly published in ways that preserve those distinctions; see, for example, James Pritchard's *Ancient Near Eastern Texts Relating to the Old Testament*[41] or Bart Ehrman's *The New Testament and Other Early Christian Writings: A Reader.*[42] It would, of course, be possible to dissolve the canonical boundaries of the Old Testament and merge Israel's scriptures with the other ancient Near Eastern writings—without any change of content

40. It is well established that Israel's sages drew on international traditions of wisdom thinking and writing, which they adapted to their own context for their own purposes. One distinct section within Proverbs (22:17–24:22) has verbal parallels with the Egyptian Instruction of Amenemopet, an earlier text (ca. 1200↓); the likelihood is that the biblical writer has drawn on the Egyptian document.

41. 3rd ed., Princeton: Princeton University Press, 1969. More recent compilations tend to substitute "Hebrew Bible" for "Old Testament" but still maintain the canonical distinction; see, e.g., Christopher Hays's *Hidden Riches: A Sourcebook for the Comparative Study of the Hebrew Bible and Ancient Near East.*

42. New York: Oxford University Press, 1998.

from Pritchard's collection, other than to add some or all of the biblical documents—and publish the whole as, say, *Ancient Near Eastern Texts*. Or one could merge the New Testament documents with the other writings from their wider world and publish them as, say, *Religious Documents from the Mediterranean World in the Time of Early Christianity*.[43] But one imagines that collections thus named would arouse less interest and attract fewer sales. If the biblical documents are classified as ancient history, then they are presumably of limited interest to readers who are not ancient historians or just intellectually curious.

Perhaps unsurprisingly, proposals to change the canon (at least of the New Testament) have been made in recent years. In *Searching the Scriptures, Vol. 2: A Feminist Commentary*,[44] familiar New Testament documents are commented upon according to their genre, alongside other ancient documents of similar genre. The editor, Elisabeth Schüssler Fiorenza, offers as a rationale: "This commentary seeks to transgress canonical boundaries in order both to undo the exclusionary kyriarchal tendencies of the ruling canon and to renew the debate on the limits, function, and extent of the canon." However, there is no attempt to offer an explicitly alternative New Testament. As Schüssler Fiorenza puts it: "This transgressive approach . . . does *not* seek to establish a new *feminist* canon. Its aim is not constructive but deconstructive. . . . Its goal is not a rehabilitation of the canon but an increase in historical-religious knowledge and imagination."[45]

But a recent attempt has in fact been made by a "New Orleans Council" of scholars and religious leaders explicitly to extend the boundaries of the New Testament and to add to it ten further documents (mostly from among those found at Nag Hammadi in the mid-twentieth century), documents commonly (whether rightly or wrongly) labeled "gnostic." The collection retains the resonant terms "New Testament" and "Bible" in its title: *A New New Testament: A Bible for the 21st Century Combining Traditional and Newly Discovered Texts*.[46] Its editor, Hal Taussig, describes it as "an explicitly alternative version of the New Testament."[47] Since the New Orleans Council

43. This is in fact what Ehrman does in his book, but he retains the canonical distinction in his title.

44. Elisabeth Schüssler Fiorenza, ed., *Searching the Scriptures, Vol. 2: A Feminist Commentary* (London: SCM, 1995).

45. Schüssler Fiorenza, *Searching the Scriptures*, 5, 8–9.

46. *A New New Testament: A Bible for the 21st Century Combining Traditional and Newly Discovered Texts*, ed. Hal Taussig (Boston and New York: Houghton Mifflin Harcourt, 2013).

47. Taussig, *New New Testament*, 509.

was self-appointed, and since this new collection has neither sponsorship
nor recognition from any recognized church, the use of "New Testament"
and "Bible" is an interestingly polemical claim. It remains to be seen what
readership and impact *A New New Testament* will attain.[48]

The basic point is that canon and religious community are
intertwined concepts. It was initially ancient Jews who compiled and privileged a collection of their sacred writings, which
ancient Christians subsequently adopted for themselves and to
which they added new sacred writings related to Jesus. Unless
one is willing in some way to grant recognition to these ancient
decisions as wise and valid, it is difficult to see how one can
continue to privilege the Bible as a distinct collection today,
other than for purely cultural (or nostalgic) reasons. The point
has been nicely put by Robert Jenson:

> Apart from the canon's role as a collection of texts the church
> assembled to serve its specific needs, the volume comprising
> the canon is not a plausible literary or historical unit, and no
> one would be reading it nor would I be writing about it. Apart
> from the fact that Israel's Scripture funded the initial church,
> and apart from the fact that the church collected writings of
> its own in one book with this Scripture, there would have been
> no "Holy Bible," and there would be no reason to treat the
> documents now bound together under that title as anything
> but sundry relics of two or more ancient Mideastern religions.
> It is only because the church maintains the collection of these
> documents, with the texts they presented, as the book she needs,
> that we are concerned for their interpretation.[49]

And again:

48. I have offered a profile and appraisal of the book in my "Canon and Religious
Truth: An Appraisal of *A New New Testament*," in *When Texts Are Canonized*, ed.
Timothy Lim, BJS (Atlanta: SBL Press, 2017), 108–35.
49. Robert Jenson, *Canon and Creed*, Interpretation: Resources for the Use of
Scripture in the Church (Louisville: Westminster John Knox, 2010), 55.

Protestantism emphasizes that these precise documents *impose* themselves on the church; Catholicism East and West emphasizes that it is the *church* that recognizes the exigency. I mean only to make the simple point presupposed by and included in both emphases: the collection comes together in and for the church.

Where the church's calling to speak the gospel is not shared, the binding of these particular documents between one cover becomes a historical accident of no hermeneutical significance.[50]

The loss of the hermeneutical significance of the canon is no small matter. On the one hand, in formal terms, the canon of Israel's scriptures is inseparably linked with the Jewish people's identity as Israel, the people of the LORD. The apostolic writings that become the New Testament express Christian belief in Jesus as Savior of the world, with the church being called to serve and bear witness to this. The combining of the New Testament with Israel's scriptures as Old Testament indicates the Christian belief that Jesus "fulfills" Israel's scriptures and is the incarnation of the God of Israel.

On the other hand, in existential and interpretive terms, the biblical canon, in the context of the continuing life and witness of the church, creates assumptions and expectations within its (would-be) Christian readers: *here* truth about God, the world, and ourselves is to be found. Not least is the critical working assumption that the God of the Old Testament is to be thought of not in the same way as Zeus/Jupiter, but rather as the one true God—the point highlighted by, and irritating to, Dawkins and Clines. This working assumption, and the difference it makes, is clearly articulated by Brevard Childs:

50. Robert Jenson, "Hermeneutics and the Life of the Church," in *Reclaiming the Bible for the Church*, ed. Carl Braaten and Robert Jenson (Edinburgh: T&T Clark, 1995), 89.

I do not come to the Old Testament to learn about someone else's God, but about the God we confess, who made himself known to Israel, to Abraham, Isaac and to Jacob. I do not approach some ancient concept, some mythological construct akin to Zeus or Moloch, but our God, our Father. The Old Testament bears witness that God revealed himself to Abraham, and we confess that he has also broken into our lives. I do not come to the Old Testament to be informed about some strange religious phenomenon, but in faith I strive for knowledge as I seek to understand ourselves in the light of God's self-disclosure. In the context of the church's scripture I seek to be pointed to our God who has made himself known, is making himself known, and will make himself known. . . . Thus, I cannot act as if I were living at the beginning of Israel's history, but as one who already knows the story, and who has entered into the middle of an activity of faith long in progress.[51]

The significance of the New Testament canon is also strongly articulated by Andrew Louth:

We become Christians by becoming members of the Church, by *trusting* our forefathers in the faith. If we cannot trust the Church to have understood Jesus, then we have lost Jesus: and the resources of modern scholarship will not help us to find him.[52]

Although one can quibble over the wording and nuance of both Childs and Louth, they each express a core Christian conviction that is exemplified and appropriated especially in contexts of worship, where people hear and pray the Scriptures of both Testaments. For present purposes, the point is that

51. Brevard S. Childs, *Old Testament Theology in a Canonical Context* (London: SCM, 1985), 28–29.
52. Andrew Louth, *Discerning the Mystery: An Essay on the Nature of Theology* (Oxford: Clarendon, 1983), 93.

expectations of finding the true God and the living Jesus in and through the Christian Bible are bound up with the privileging of certain writings, but not others, as constituting this Bible. Whatever debates continue to surround this recognition, it is important to see what is at stake. The truth value of the Bible as Bible is inseparable from recognition of the church as its plausibility structure.

One further observation may be made in relation to a particular issue within biblical scholarship. It is a commonplace for biblical scholars to object to any notion that faith might be a requirement for biblical study. Faith is irrelevant, for what is needed is the acquiring of the necessary philological and historical skills and their disciplined and honest use so as to follow the evidence of the texts where it leads, and this can be done by anyone who is interested and capable of doing the work. Faith is also discriminatory, for there is a dismaying history in the seventeenth to nineteenth centuries of religious tests as entrance requirements for academic and political eligibility, whereby Jews, atheists, and others were excluded. That legitimate academic study should be blind to issues of personal faith became a core understanding of modernity, and is part of what is implied by the default status of the historical-critical approach in biblical scholarship. The general sweeping away of faith-related discrimination is gain, and no one should want to put the clock back.

My concern here is not the postmodern recognition that faith convictions are not the only complicating factor that might affect how one reads the biblical text—for the "masters of suspicion," Marx, Freud, and Nietzsche, have highlighted the complex and variegated factors that bear upon all interpretation, whether of the Bible or anything else. Moreover, ideological convictions of one kind or another can have an impact comparable to that of faith convictions (even if they have not been formally institutionalized in the same way that Christian convictions once were). Rather, my question concerns faith in the sense of an antecedent ecclesial understanding that individuals appropriate when they become Christians. The privileging of selected documents as part of the biblical canon is an ecclesial faith decision. Or, put differently, the biblical canon is a confessional construct, and the recognition of the biblical deity as the true God is an ecclesial belief. There has been a certain oddity in the way some scholars have opposed any notion of faith in an individual sense while apparently not thinking twice about accepting the privileging of certain documents via the concept of canon (they have directed their labors to writing commentaries only on canonical books), and accepting as a working assumption that the biblical deity is the one true God (they have spoken of the biblical deity as "God," not "a god," in a way that is warranted only by the Jewish and Christian faiths). That is, they have approached the text with assumptions generated and warranted by Christian faith and theology. However, this situation is slowly changing; one can increasingly find commentaries on noncanonical books, and scholars—even Christian scholars—are increasingly using the form "god" rather than "God."

The modern paradigm of biblical scholarship thinks in terms of what is necessary for the individual scholar to be an informed and honest scholar. Well and good. However, the characteristic assumption that there is no necessary link between the knowledge one articulates and the habits of thought and practices of life one adopts is surely open to question; the character of the interpreter makes a difference to the nature and quality of interpretation that is produced. Moreover, as already noted, attention to the social nature of knowledge calls into question the modern privileging of individualism and rationalism and requires a fundamental reframing of how biblical study should be understood and practiced. What the future paradigms of biblical study will look like, no one knows. My own hope is that it will be possible—while still maintaining the appropriateness of every kind of responsible approach to studying the biblical text—to develop modes of study that more robustly reintegrate the academic study of the Bible with the ongoing thought and practices of Christian faith (and also, allowing for all differences, with those of Judaism), and thereby bring the biblical visions of God and life into constructive and critical engagement with other contemporary visions of the world.

The Case Study: Ancient Reception and Interpretation of *Aeneid* 1 and Daniel 7

Both *Aeneid* 1 and Daniel 7 continued to be significant long after their context of origin receded into history. The *Aeneid* became a core element in Roman culture and education, while Daniel became a part of Israel's sacred scriptures and thereby part of Jewish education and formation. Both *Aeneid* 1 and Daniel 7 belong to larger works that were treated by Romans and Jews respectively as presenting privileged perspectives for understanding the world and their position in it. The continuing life of the Roman and Jewish people in antiquity provided something of a plausibility structure for being responsive to the content of these privileged documents. And in contemporary Western culture, which has been historically shaped by Roman and Jewish influences (among others), there are good reasons for engaging with these documents as still in some way significant; each is a classic, though for Jews and Christians, Daniel 7 is also Scripture.

To put it differently, thus far we have considered "the world within the text" in relation to "the world behind the text," but it is now time to include "the world in front of the text"—that is, those communities and people who have looked to, and in significant ways identified with, the content of these works as they read and appropriated them in contexts beyond those of their origins.

The Reception of the Aeneid and "Limitless Empire" in Roman Antiquity

"The celebrity of Virgil's works in the Roman world was immediate and lasting."[53] Both the quality of the poetry and the nature of Virgil's poetic vision were understandably congenial to the people of Rome, who could imaginatively construe their own identity and position in light of the poem. Knowledge of Virgil's phrases and images became ubiquitous; for example, there are numerous Virgilian graffiti on the walls of Pompeii, which was reduced to ruin by the eruption of Mount Vesuvius in 79↑, about a century after Virgil's death. But Virgil also quickly gained a quasi-religious significance, as in the *sortes Virgilianae*, the practice of inquiring about the future by opening the text

53. R. J. Tarrant, "Aspects of Virgil's Reception in Antiquity," in *The Cambridge Companion to Virgil*, ed. Charles Martindale (Cambridge: Cambridge University Press, 1997), 56.

of Virgil at random and seeing what caught the eye—a practice that was already undertaken by the emperor Hadrian in the second century↑ (and is even said also to have been carried out in the seventeenth century by King Charles I during the English Civil War).[54]

The widespread popularity of the *Aeneid* is in itself no guide to precisely how people understood its content. But it remains a reasonable judgment that the vision of unlimited empire did not cease to be congenial to ancient Romans. In terms of the understanding of Virgil's vision for the first three to three and a half centuries after its composition, there is perhaps little to say other than that its vision of Rome became a core element in Roman identity.

Nonetheless, there is an interesting question to ask about what happened when the frame of reference within which Virgil was read changed at a fundamental level. When the Roman Empire adopted the Christian faith, how was Virgil understood?

Generally speaking, historic Christian reception of Virgil has been strongly positive. Already at the end of the second century↑, Tertullian famously spoke of Virgil as displaying a "naturally Christian spirit" (*anima naturaliter Christiana*).[55] And Dante's assigning Virgil a role as his guide in the *Divine Comedy* attests a strong sense of the congruity of Virgil's vision with that of Christian faith (even while the recognition that Virgil was not a Christian restricted how far he could guide Dante). But the specific difference that was made to a reading of Virgil's "limitless empire" in Late Antiquity is less evident in the literature than it might be, because the focus of Christian interest, in both ancient sources and modern studies, has been much less on the *Aeneid* than on one of Virgil's ten pastoral poems (the "eclogues")—specifically, the Fourth Eclogue.

54. Primary evidence is helpfully collected in Helen A. Loane's "The *Sortes Vergilianae*," *Classical Weekly* 21, no. 24 (1928): 185–89.
55. Tertullian, *Apology* 17.

In the Fourth Eclogue, Virgil speaks in lyrical—and in a sense, "apocalyptic"—terms of a boy, apparently just born (though perhaps about to be born). With the appearance of this boy, the world is transformed with the coming of a new Golden Age:

> Ours is the crowning era foretold in prophecy:
> Born of Time, a great new cycle of centuries
> Begins. Justice returns to earth, the Golden Age
> Returns, and its first-born comes down from heaven above.
>   (*Eclogue* 4.4–7)[56]
> [*Ultima Cumaei venit iam carminis aetas;*
> *magnus ab integro saeclorum nascitur ordo:*
> *iam redit et virgo, redeunt Saturnia regna;*
> *iam nova progenies caelo demittitur alto.*]

In terms of the world behind the text, some specific information is given within the poem: it is addressed to Pollio, a friend of Virgil who had just been appointed consul. Although the identity of the boy is not specified, and so cannot be known for sure (and many candidates have been proposed), it is perhaps most likely that this is Pollio's son, and that the occasion for the poem was this son's birth. The precise register of the language is hard to catch at this distance, though without too much difficulty it can be read as good-natured hyperbole in congratulation of the happy events of consulship and fatherhood coinciding, and saying, in effect, "Great things lie ahead."

But when a reading of the world within the text no longer takes its bearings from the originating world behind the text, the language of the poem is open to be read otherwise. There is perhaps a certain appropriateness in the fact that it seems to have been the emperor Constantine, who inaugurated the process by which Christianity eventually became the official religion of the Roman Empire, who also was the first to offer a distinctively Christian reading of the Fourth Eclogue. In an oration that may well have been delivered as a Good Friday sermon to a council of bishops and theologians at Antioch in 325,[57] Constantine speaks, among other things, about Virgil as a kind of prophet of the Christian faith. He reads the poem "messianically," in a way not dissimilar to some Christian readings of the Old Testament,

56. I am using the helpfully interpretive rendering of C. Day Lewis, *The Eclogues, Georgics and Aeneid of Virgil* (London: Oxford University Press, 1966), 18.

57. The document is the "Oration to the Saints," which comes at the end of Eusebius's *Life of Constantine*. Full details, together with an engaging account of this proposed scenario, are provided by Robin Lane Fox, *Pagans and Christians* (Harmondsworth, UK: Viking, 1986), 627–56.

as looking to a great future that is realized in the coming of Christ. The impact of this reading has been enormous. But it is not our present concern.

Nonetheless, some Christian engagement with the *Aeneid*'s vision of "limitless empire" is what one would expect, and this indeed can be found. I take two representative, and interestingly contrasting, examples: Prudentius and Augustine.

Prudentius (348–ca. 413) was a significant Latin Christian poet who lived through the time in which Christianity was adopted as the official religion of the Roman Empire, and who felt it important to produce a positive Christian alternative to traditional and still-persisting pagan perspectives. He followed the precedent of others, especially Constantine's biographer Eusebius, in developing the idea that the history of Rome was a kind of "preparation for the gospel," and that Rome would attain its greatest glory now that it had become Christian. R. A. Markus sketches this view thus: "The Empire founded by Augustus was the providentially established vehicle of Christianity, and the history of the period since the Incarnation (under Augustus!) could be read as the progressive realisation of divine purpose. The spreading and establishing of Christianity over the world, inaugurated under Augustus, was being completed under the Christian emperors of the fourth century."[58]

In ca. 401–3 Prudentius wrote a poem as a resistant response to an appeal for the tolerance of paganism by Symmachus, a respected prefect of Rome. In the course of his poem, Prudentius uses Virgil's words about "limitless empire" in a somewhat surprising way. He refers to Catiline's conspiracy in 63↓ and Cicero's role in rescuing Rome from this conspiracy, a moment in Roman history that had already clearly achieved paradigmatic status as threat to Rome and deliverance—apparently somewhat analogous to the classic significance, in English history, of the

58. R. A. Markus, *Saeculum: History and Society in the Theology of St. Augustine* (Cambridge: Cambridge University Press, 1970), 161–62.

Spanish Armada of 1588. Prudentius depicts the deliverance of Rome through Cicero as exemplifying Rome's destiny to have lasting dominion, and so uses Virgil's words with reference to Cicero's(!) achievement:

> No bounds he set, no limits fixed of time;
> An empire without end he showed, lest power
> And glory won by Rome should ever wane. (*Against Symmachus* 1.541–43)
> [*Denique nec metas statuit nec tempora ponit,
> imperium sine fine docet, ne Romula virtus
> iam sit anus, norit ne gloria parta senectam.*]

Prudentius also sees Rome's imperial role in the world as now taken up and realized in Christ, who brings together Rome's rule with peace for the earth:

> Come then, Almighty, to this peaceful earth!
> The world united now by peace and Rome
> Possesses Thee, O Christ. These two you will
> To rule all things, but not Rome without peace.
>   (*Against Symmachus* 2.634–37)[59]

It is not hard to see why such an appropriation of Virgil's vision might have been attractive to many Christians in Rome, who hoped that Christ would bring the realization of what Virgil had spoken of and that had not yet been realized: an empire of true peace. There is clear value in such a moral vision. Unfortunately, it is also not hard to read Prudentius as being complacent and blinkered. Not least among many factors is that within less than a decade of Prudentius's writing, the warfare

59. I am using the translation by Sister M. Clement Eagan, CCVI, in *The Poems of Prudentius*, vol. 2, FC (Washington, DC: Catholic University of America Press, 1962), 133, 160. The Latin text is taken from *Aurelii Prudentii Clementis Carmina*, ed. M. P. Cunningham, CCSL 126 (Turnholt: Brepols, 1966), 204.

that was rumbling at the time of his writing culminated, in 410, in Rome being sacked for the first time in its history, as its enemies, led by Alaric the Visigoth, were triumphant.

Augustine's approach to Rome and its empire is more searching. Unsurprisingly, he too draws on Virgil (among many other resources), since Augustine as an educated citizen of the empire had a long history of reading and reflecting on Virgil (probably best known in relation to his *Confessions*).[60] The sack of Rome in 410 produced an existential crisis for many in the Roman Empire. Although the empire was now officially Christian, many nonetheless asked whether the downfall of the city might have been caused by their abandonment of their previous deities: Might turning to Christ have been the problem rather than the solution? Augustine responds to this deep existential question at length in *City of God*, but there is an illuminating prelude to *City of God* in a sermon he preached in Carthage in 411, in the almost-immediate aftermath of Alaric's sack of Rome.

In this address, Sermon 105,[61] Augustine wants nothing to do with the stance taken by Prudentius. Initially Augustine speaks in a general way about the importance of hope. He then turns to the specific issue of Rome's overthrow. Here he contrasts earthly kingdoms with the heavenly kingdom: "Why panic, just because earthly kingdoms crumble? That's why a heavenly kingdom was promised to you, so that you wouldn't crumble away with the earthly ones." Having sounded

60. A still-useful older work on Augustine's reading of Virgil, which both cites texts and offers analysis, is Harald Hagendahl's *Augustine and the Latin Classics*, 2 vols. (Göteborg: Elanders Bohtryckeri Aktiebolag, 1967). A succinct recent treatment is Gary Wills's "Vergil and St. Augustine," in *A Companion to Vergil's Aeneid and Its Tradition*, ed. Joseph Farrell and Michael C. J. Putnam (Chichester, UK: Wiley-Blackwell, 2010), 123–32.

61. I am using the translation of Sermon 105 in *Sermons*, trans. Edmund Hill, OP, ed. John E. Rotelle, OSA, The Works of Saint Augustine III/4 (Brooklyn: New City Press, 1992), 88–98, esp. 93–94. The passages I cite are from paragraphs 9 and 10, on pp. 93–94.

this note, he moves directly to a seemingly scornful attack on Virgil:

> Those who made such a promise to earthly kingdoms were not governed by the truth but were lying in order to flatter. One of their poets brought in Jupiter speaking, and had him say of the Romans:
>
> > To these I set no bounds of space or time;
> > Dominion without end have I bestowed.
>
> That, obviously, is not the answer that truth gives. . . .

Interestingly, however, Augustine then goes on to imagine a dialogue with Virgil in which he envisages Virgil offering a threefold defense of his famous words: he had to cope with the pressures put on a poet to say what people wanted to hear, he of course knew that Jupiter was not a true god, and elsewhere in his poetry he did in fact recognize that Rome's empire was not limitless. Thus:

> Perhaps if we wanted to taunt Virgil about this, and tease him for saying such a thing, he would put up with us to some extent, and say to us, "Yes, I too know this perfectly well; but what was I to do? I used to earn my living by selling words to the Romans, so I had to flatter them by promising something that wasn't true. And yet even here I was canny; when I said 'Dominion without end have I bestowed,' I brought in their Jupiter to say it. I didn't utter a falsehood in my own person, but I imposed the mask of falsehood on Jupiter; just as he was a false god, so was he a lying soothsayer. But do you want to see that I knew all this? In another place, when I didn't bring in Jupiter as a talking stone [i.e., an oracle], but spoke in my own person, I said,
>
> > Nor Roman state, and kingdoms doomed to die. [*Georgics* 2.498]

Observe that I said 'kingdoms doomed to die.' I said that kingdoms were doomed to die, I didn't keep quiet about it."

Augustine then sums up in a way that affirms the basic
truthfulness of Virgil and thereby softens, without denying,
the critique that in the famous lines about limitless empire
Virgil was speaking untruthfully: "That [earthly kingdoms]
would crumble to dust, he didn't hide, for the sake of truth;
that they would remain for ever, he promised out of flattery"
(Sermon 105.10). The power of the earthly city of Rome is
not limitless, unlike that of the heavenly city. But Virgil, whom
Augustine respects so deeply, really knew this anyway—or so
Augustine contends.

In *City of God* one would naturally expect Augustine to be
dismissive of "limitless empire" in much the same way that he
is in Sermon 105. At the very outset, in the preface, Augustine
refers to those words of Anchises that are so regularly paired
with those of Jupiter—"sparing the conquered, striking down
the haughty" (*Aen.* 6.853)[62]—and treats them dismissively as
an example of human pride arrogating to itself the power and
mercy that belong to God alone. Yet in a striking passage at
the end of book 2, where he is urging the Romans to abandon
false gods and turn to the true God, Augustine says this:

Now reach out and grasp the heavenly homeland . . . in which
you will reign truly and eternally. There will be no Vestal hearth
for you there, no Capitoline stone [an ancient statue of Jupiter, whose temple on the Capitol had historically been Rome's
primary temple], but the one true God, who "will confine your
fortunes within no boundaries or durations, but will give empire
without end." (*City of God* 2.29)[63]

62. See above, ch. 2, p. 57.
63. I am using the translation by William Babcock in *The City of God*, ed. Boniface Ramsey, The Works of Saint Augustine I/6 (New York: New City Press, 2012).

Here, remarkably, Augustine takes the famous words from the lips of Jupiter and ascribes them to the one true God. Augustine's understanding is that the only limitless empire of which these words can truly be said is that over which the God who is known in Jesus Christ reigns; however, this is no longer an earthly Rome, as in Prudentius, but a heavenly homeland. That Augustine feels it appropriate to take these words and reuse them in this way is testimony to the enduring imaginative impact of "limitless empire" and the way in which this notion could be appropriated by Christians, even as its referent was transformed.

There is thus a mixed reception of Virgil in Late Antiquity. The *Aeneid* remained a privileged document, into whose perspectives both pagan Romans and then Christian Romans sought to enter, and whose content both pagans and Christians sought to appropriate. Prudentius and many others found it natural to suppose that a Christian Roman Empire might fulfill God's purposes for the world. Augustine, however, sees more deeply into the perspectives of the Bible as a whole when he keeps a strong critical distance between human dominion and the kingdom of God, and when he comes to deny any special significance to the Roman Empire in God's purposes. R. A. Markus sums up Augustine's mature attitude thus:

> The Empire has become no more than a historical, empirical society with a chequered career. . . . It is theologically neutral. . . . The only clue to sacred history is the Bible. Where this is silent, human guesswork about divine purposes in history lacks foundation. The Christianisation of the Roman Empire is as accidental to the history of salvation as it is reversible; there is nothing definitive about the *christiana tempora*, we can have no assurance that an age of persecutions will not return.[64]

64. Markus, *Saeculum*, 55, 54.

For Augustine, "limitless empire" has become empty on its own terms, and is meaningful only if transformed through transposition into a Christ-centered frame of reference.

The Reception of Daniel 7 in Jewish Antiquity

I want to approach the reception of Daniel 7 through a consideration of some distinct but related interpretive issues that complexify our initial reading of the biblical text. Thus far I have assumed that the vision of Daniel 7 originally in some way related to Jewish hopes of a successful resistance to Antiochus Epiphanes's oppression, and I have suggested that it appears to be a Jewish counterpart to the Roman vision of *Aeneid* 1.

If the two visions are considered together, one might perhaps say that a significant difference between them relates to the context from which each vision is formulated. While the vision of empire in *Aeneid* 1 comes from the rulers, the powerful, the vision of Daniel 7 comes from the ruled, those with little power. Yet although that clearly is a real difference, how best should it be understood? We know from 1 Maccabees something of the conflict that surrounded Antiochus's assault on the symbols of Jewish identity. In light of that, one can easily assume that the "dominion" of Daniel 7 must be the same kind of dominion that Antiochus was seeking to impose. Thus it could be said that although Daniel 7 comes from those with little power, they did gain power for a while; the problem was that it was limited to their own independence, which over time they lost again. The underlying attitude to power and dominion over others therefore could be the same in each vision, but the Jews, unlike the Romans, were much less successful in attaining it.

This brings us, however, to a major interpretive difficulty that I have glossed over so far: What is really envisaged by the dominion that the Ancient One bestows? What does it mean when read within the book of Daniel as a whole? As already seen, in Daniel 7 there is a stark contrast between the four beasts, two of which devour and destroy, and the figure "like a human being" to whom dominion is transferred from the beasts. Since the four beasts explicitly represent four kingdoms/kings, the vision envisages a contrast not between animals and humans but between humans who behave like savage animals and humans who, by implication, behave humanly/humanely. It is these latter who receive everlasting dominion from the Ancient One on the throne.

What it means to behave humanly/humanely is not spelled out in the vision and so has to be inferred from the wider literary context of the book. In terms of the narratives in the first half of the book of Daniel, the human qualities displayed and commended are primarily faithfulness and integrity in adversity (Dan. 1) and a loyalty to God even in the face of death (Dan. 3; 6)—though there is also a portrayal of Daniel as possessing wisdom greater than that of his Babylonian captors (Dan. 2; 4; 5). Similarly, in the most extensive scene in the second half of the book, the angelic account to Daniel of heavenly and earthly conflicts around Daniel's people, oppression is to be met by "people who are loyal to [yāda', "know"] their God" and who "stand firm and take action," even if death will come to some of them, including the wise (11:32–35). Thus, in relation to the vision of Daniel 7, the wider book portrays faithfulness and loyalty, and also wisdom, as the qualities of life expected for resisting the four beasts for as long as they have their dominion. Although a reversal is expected, in which those who endure will themselves exercise dominion, the nature of that dominion is nowhere specified but is implicitly the sovereignty of humans embodying a strong understanding of faithfulness and wisdom.

Put differently: a striking peculiarity of the book of Daniel is that it depicts no fighting, no military action on the part of Daniel or other faithful Jews, even in prospect. When it speaks of the wise falling by the sword and suffering captivity and plunder (Dan. 11:33), no mention is made of action on a battlefield and/or striking back at the enemy. No hope is expressed of a Jewish hand, or any human hand, contributing to the end of Antiochus Epiphanes, about whom the last thing said is simply that "he shall come to his end, with no one to help him" (11:45). Moreover, the note of hope on which the book ends is not a picture of Jews ruling over others but the hope that "many shall be purified, cleansed, and refined" and awake from death to everlasting life (11:35; 12:2, 10).[65]

One way of posing the interpretive challenge is the question of how much weight should be given to "the world within the text" in relation to "the world behind the text." How far should one allow the background context of the Jewish struggle against Antiochus Epiphanes to affect a reading of the book of Daniel's own portrayal of resistance and hopes for the future? Is the primary imaginative framework for reading Daniel 7 the extensive accounts of military resistance in 1 Maccabees, or is it the literary context of the book of Daniel as a whole, which says nothing about military resistance? And if, in some way, both contexts should be brought to bear, then how best should they be held together and interrelated?

Over against a reading of Daniel 7 in relation to 1 Maccabees, a recent summary account of Daniel 7–12 offers a differently weighted reading by relating the biblical text to other ancient works from the literary genre of "apocalyptic":

> The visions of Daniel 7–12 disclose a heavenly world and an imminent culmination to history. They contain pulsing images on a mythic scale; they predict the ultimate triumph of good over evil. A steady increase of worldwide evil is inevitable, according to the visions, but there will follow an end-time triumph of God

65. See further Daniel L. Smith-Christopher, "The Book of Daniel," in *The New Interpreter's Bible*, ed. Leander E. Keck (Nashville: Abingdon, 1996), 7:17–152, esp. "Excursus: Daniel and Nonviolence" (144–46).

over its forces. God is about to intervene in history, destroying the dehumanizing spirit embedded within the world's empires. When that happens, God will overthrow wholesale all imperial systems of control, establish an everlasting dominion on earth, and reward the faithful.[66]

Does Daniel 7–12 depict victory over Antiochus Epiphanes? Or the ultimate triumph of good over evil? Are these two identical? Or are they quite distinct? Or does the former in some way embody and anticipate the latter? Which way should the interpretive imagination go?

> Later rabbinic tradition offers another imaginative option, closer in spirit to Daniel than to Maccabees but distinct from both. This was to relate the eight days of Hanukkah (the festival of the rededication of the temple after its desecration by Antiochus Epiphanes) to a miracle within the temple that resonated with biblical imagery of God's provision and presence: "When the Greeks entered the Temple, they defiled all the oils therein, and when the Hasmonean dynasty prevailed against and defeated them, they made search and found only one cruse of oil which lay with the seal of the High Priest, but which contained sufficient [oil] for one day's lighting only; yet a miracle was wrought therein and they lit [the lamp] therewith for eight days. The following year these [days] were appointed a Festival with [the recital of] Hallel and thanksgiving."[67]

There are thus acute problems having to do with the interpretation of the vision and religious language of Daniel 7. Although there are excellent reasons for relating the vision of the heavenly court to the historical context of the Maccabean Revolt, the question of precisely how they relate is simply unclear and open to more than one reading. In this sense there is a much greater intrinsic density to the language and vision of

66. Stephen L. Cook, "Apocalyptic Writings," in *The Cambridge Companion to the Hebrew Bible / Old Testament*, ed. Stephen B. Chapman and Marvin A. Sweeney (New York: Cambridge University Press, 2016), 331.

67. See b. Shabbat 21b, in *The Babylonian Talmud: Seder Mo'ed*, vol. 1, *Shabbath*, ed. I. Epstein (London: Soncino, 1938), 92–93.

Daniel 7 than there is in *Aeneid* 1. A good case can be made for the thesis that the book of Daniel as a whole, in its own right, is subverting any straightforward notion of dominion and is reconceiving where, under the God of Israel, true power and dominion lie.

A further interpretive issue relates to understanding Daniel 7 in the context of the canonical preservation of the book as a whole. For canonical preservation—the locating of Daniel alongside other books recognized as sacred and authoritative, and its being read together with them—of necessity involves recontextualization. A literary and socioreligious context, of a collection of documents being read in and for a continuing community, in certain ways displaces the original historical context, even if, of course, the evidence for that originating context remains within the documents.

How, then, was Daniel 7 understood as the Maccabean crisis receded into history? The short answer is: we know little.[68] Yet it seems clear that, for whatever reasons, the book of Daniel was not considered to have "gotten it wrong" (perhaps because Jews had not achieved dominion over their neighbors, or because the kingdom of God and the end time of history had not arrived?) and thereby relegated to the margins of Jewish history.[69] Rather,

68. For discussion, see Lester L. Grabbe, "A Dan(iel) for All Seasons: For Whom Was Daniel Important?," in *The Book of Daniel: Composition and Reception*, ed. John J. Collins and Peter W. Flint (Leiden: Brill, 2002), 1:229–46, esp. 236–39, 244; and Klaus Koch, "Stages in the Canonization of the Book of Daniel," in *The Book of Daniel: Composition and Reception*, ed. John J. Collins and Peter W. Flint (Leiden: Brill, 2002), 2:421–46.

69. This working assumption that Daniel was not considered to have "gotten it wrong" is interestingly challenged by Michael Satlow in the essay "Bad Prophecies: Canon and the Case of the Book of Daniel," in *When Texts Are Canonized*, ed. Timothy Lim (Atlanta: SBL Press, 2017), 63–81. Satlow argues that the content of Daniel was initially known only within limited scholastic circles, which may simply have preserved the material for antiquarian reasons. Only after enough time had passed, and the inaccuracy of the text was no longer seen for what it was, did the book gain widespread recognition, when its content was considered applicable to the Jews' relationship with Rome. This is a possible scenario. But Satlow's argument

it was preserved as part of Israel's authoritative writings, even when Hellenistic dominion over the Jewish people was eventually replaced by Roman dominion.

At least two key interpretive moves appear to have been made in the understanding of Daniel 7 as it was preserved. First, it appears that, whatever particular realization the vision may have received in the context of the Maccabean Revolt, its full realization was understood to be something that remained for the future, as yet to come about at some subsequent date.

> This is in accord with what appears to have been the way of understanding some of the material elsewhere in the Old Testament that has strong resonances with Daniel 7—that is, God's promise to David of an unending dynasty. The primary articulation of this is Nathan's oracle to David in 2 Samuel 7, when David is told that he cannot build a house (i.e., temple) for the LORD, but that the LORD would build a house (i.e., dynasty) for David, and that this dynasty would explicitly have no termination but be "in perpetuity" / "without end" ('ad 'ōlām, 2 Sam. 7:13, 16). The end of the Davidic dynasty in the fall of Jerusalem to the Babylonians in 587↓ did not lead to an abandoning of the Davidic hope in Israel's scriptures but to its reenvisioning—the shorthand for which is the phenomenon of "messianic" expectation.

If its realization was projected into the future, that implies something about the value of the vision thus projected: it matters so much that it is not simply to be set aside or written off. Of course, such a move can be read in more than one way. It can easily be read unsympathetically in terms of cognitive dissonance and an inability to accept that a cherished hope had proved mistaken, and thus as a rationalization of the limited post-Maccabean dominion of the Hasmoneans as a delay yet awaiting further fulfillment (which can easily be depicted as wishful thinking, fantasy, and so forth). Of course, there

---

depends on a rather wooden notion of prophetic "authenticity" that has no place for the articulation of a moral and religious vision of reality having its own validity for those who receive it.

may have been dimensions of such refusal and rationalization. However, conjectures about mind-sets in such situations remain just that: conjectures. Moreover, we have already seen that the question of what might count as a fulfillment of Daniel 7 is intrinsically unstraightforward.

Material that relates to basic life issues and a vision of God is likely to be valued in complex ways and on more than one level. In other words, the content of the vision of Daniel 7 was seen to represent a basic hope and aspect of self-understanding on the part of those who preserved it. It came to constitute an expression of the moral vision of its community, in which hope for the future takes the form of an unspecified dominion to be given—ultimately—by God to those who are both faithful and holy, and who resist other humans who oppress them and try to make them forgo their identity and allegiance.

> An early interpretation of the book of Daniel, perhaps from the last decades of the first century↓, can be found in the Qumran War Rule (1QM) (a complex and difficult writing).[70] This makes no reference to Daniel 7 but rather draws on the pictures of the coming end in Daniel 10–12. The time of crisis and resolution depicted in Daniel is transposed to the context of the Qumran community. Whatever the precise nature of the community's expectations of the realization of the biblical material in their context, it is clear that they see its content as requiring faithfulness in the struggle between the spirits of Light and of Darkness.

A second interpretive move relates to the fact that the identity of the fearsome beasts was seen to be open to continuing reflection. In part this may have been because the text of Daniel 7 itself emphasizes not the identity of the beasts (it does not "identify" them at all) but rather their fearsome qualities. Even

70. The material is conveniently available in, e.g., *The Dead Sea Scrolls in English*, trans. G. Vermes, 4th ed. (Harmondsworth, UK: Penguin, 1995), 123–45. There is a parallel text of Hebrew and English in *The Dead Sea Scrolls Study Edition*, vol. 1, *1Q1–4Q273*, ed. Florentino García Martínez and Eibert J. C. Tigchelaar (Grand Rapids: Eerdmans, 1997), 112–45.

if the identity of the beasts would have been reasonably clear to the original writer and recipients—especially the final beast as the Hellenistic empire and the horn as Antiochus Epiphanes—such identification was open to change over time: a changing context for readers can lead to a changed reading. The textual imagery is intrinsically open to be applied to other kings and empires in other contexts, especially when the biblical text is read with a strong sense of existential identification with its content. When the Jewish people were forcibly incorporated into the dominion of Rome, it became natural to see the fourth beast as having a Roman identity. There is a long history of both Jews and Christians reading the passage in this way.

> As time went on, the beasts received other identifications as seemed relevant to the interpreters' context. One common Christian reading was that the offensive little horn was the antichrist, who could variously be identified as the threatening opposition of the day: Islam, the papacy—if the interpreters were Protestant—and others.

Such reapplication of the imagery of Daniel 7, as of so many other biblical passages, works, in effect, on the principle of analogy that is used with all enduring literature read with full imaginative seriousness: if the description seems applicable, then it can apply.

Conclusion

I have sought in this chapter to move beyond the initial reading of "the plain sense" of *Aeneid* 1 and Daniel 7 set out in chapter 2. The concern has been to consider the reading of these passages beyond their context of origin, as they received privileged status and ancient readers in one way or another sought to appropriate their content and live in their light. What difference does this make to readings of these passages?

In general terms, there is a dialectic between "the world within the text" and "the world in front of the text," the imaginative thought world and life of those who preserve and privilege the material. The significance of the world behind the text tends to fade as history moves on and situations change, although this can vary greatly from text to text.

For *Aeneid* 1 there appears to have been little interest on the part of ancient Romans in thinking about the specific context of Augustus's incipient imperial rule. Rather, the vision within the text of "limitless empire" for Rome captured their imagination and endured. This remained true when Rome became Christian, though there were clearly marked differences as to precisely what empire reconceived in the light of Christ might mean.

One way of putting the interpretive challenge of *Aeneid* 1 is that the vision of endless empire posed a particular temptation for Christians. A clear part of the attraction of a limitless Roman empire is that people can want to be "on the winning side"—a desire that may be self-serving but that runs deep and is not necessarily misguided. Yet how should this be handled if the truth about God and life is understood by Christians to be definitively given in Jesus, who was crucified by Rome yet raised by God? The temptation to which many, including Prudentius, succumbed was to hope that the vision of endless empire could be, as it were, baptized into Christ without too much difficulty. Augustine, by contrast, may not have had all the answers, but he wrestled more searchingly with the questions.

For Daniel 7 I have argued that an initial reading of the text in which its "everlasting dominion" is the same as Virgil's "limitless empire" needs to be reconsidered in light of the context of the book of Daniel as a whole, which seems to point in a different direction. Moreover, whatever one decides about the best sense of Daniel 7 in relation to its context of origin, its continuing reception fairly clearly steers a reading of the text towards its being a paradigmatic expression of the need for faithfulness and hope in God in recurrent situations of oppression. The "unending dominion" of Daniel 7 thus is of a different order than the "limitless empire" of *Aeneid* 1, because Daniel 7 is not speaking of any prospect of power in the same way.

In this chapter I have also noted the importance of "significant others" for entering into and embracing the particular understanding of the divine and the human expressed by privileged documents. To be impressed by, and so come to respect and perhaps also to wish to join, other people is an important factor. The appeal of the limitless empire of *Aeneid* 1 seems fairly straightforward in its ancient context. Given the reality and extent of Roman power, to become a citizen of the Roman Empire would be an obviously attractive goal for many in antiquity. The appeal of Daniel 7, however, appears to be less straightforward and more demanding. A positive appropriation of Daniel 7 would in principle entail a willingness at least to sympathize, and perhaps to identify, with a small and regularly oppressed people who have a strong commitment to faithfulness in adversity, and who through that faithfulness maintain confidence in the ultimate triumph of their vision of a just God.

This latter option, however, is again open to some reframing—or so I will argue in the next chapter.

||||||||||||||||||||||||||||

4

||||||||||||||||||||||||||||

Towards Trust and Truth

The story so far. Step 1 was to set the stage. Initially I briefly il-
lustrated both the historic importance of the Bible for Christians
and some of the typical obstacles to believing it to be a privileged vehicle of divine truth in today's world. I also suggested
that some key issues are implicit in the scholarly axiom that
one should interpret the Bible "like any other book." Responsible scholarship must indeed recognize that biblical literature
resembles other literature in both form and content, and offer
some account of this. The drawback is that this recognition easily lends itself to approaches that treat the Bible as a "merely"
human phenomenon in which the divine dimension becomes
occluded, or rather (re-)interpreted as a human construct. Com-
paring *Aeneid* 1 and Daniel 7, with their strikingly similar content, offers a specific example whereby to focus questions that
otherwise may remain somewhat abstract.

Step 2 involved setting out something of the diversity of
valid nonreligious approaches to the biblical documents, approaches that may be classified under the convenient headings

of "ancient history" and "classic." In illustration of the value
of such approaches, which entail disciplined understanding and
use of philology and history, I offered an expanded account of
Aeneid 1 and Daniel 7 in these terms.

Step 3 moved into less familiar territory. On the one hand, I
noted the general phenomenon whereby people privilege some
factors over others as providing interpretive keys for understanding the world as a whole, and I suggested that the Christian
privileging of the Bible and of Jesus is a particular instance of
this phenomenon. On the other hand, I noted the general importance of plausibility structures, and I suggested that people
are most likely to take seriously the Christian privileging of
the Bible and of Jesus if they encounter the lives of Christians
as a plausibility structure that moves them towards the Christian way of life and thought, with a possible view towards
making it their own. In line with this suggestion, I noted that
the reception and understanding of *Aeneid* 1 and Daniel 7 in
contexts beyond their context of origin were tied up with their
continuing role in the lives of Romans and Jews, and that the
reading of these texts in their reception raises awareness of
some important differences between them that may not have
been initially apparent.

However, the argument thus far is still incomplete. An emphasis on plausibility structures alone could lead some people
to say (in effect), "I find my present plausibility structure to be
satisfactory," and to see no good reason for even entertaining
the possibility of some kind of change. Alternatively, even if
people of Christian faith are seen to be a persuasive plausibility structure, this might be taken to amount to not much more
than "Join the club and make new friends; and, among other
things, try to take the Bible seriously," with little explanation
of why this club should be preferred to any other friendly club,
or what taking the Bible seriously for faith may entail. More
needs to be said about what the persuasive force of Christian

witness in the world requires if a person is to become, not just in name but in reality, someone who believes the biblical witness, and supremely its witness to Jesus—and why such belief should be a good thing.

Faith, Belief, and Religious Knowledge

Much could be said about the nature of faith in God or the meaning of belief in relation to the content of the Bible. Here I will just point in the general direction that the main road takes within a Christian frame of reference.

Richard Dawkins's Account of Belief in God

Mistakes can be instructive. I would like to set the stage with Richard Dawkins's mistaken account of belief in God in *The God Delusion*. One of his clear and emphatic claims is that the existence or nonexistence of God is a matter to be determined by science. He defines what he calls "the God hypothesis" as the contention that "there exists a superhuman, supernatural intelligence who deliberately designed and created the universe and everything in it, including us," and he says of God as thus defined:

Either he exists or he doesn't. It is a scientific question.

The existence of God is a scientific hypothesis like any other.

God's existence or non-existence is a scientific fact about the universe, discoverable in principle if not in practice.[1]

In response to the often-made point that science is not competent to adjudicate an issue such as the reality of God—Dawkins

1. Dawkins, *God Delusion*, 31, 48, 50.

cites the words of Stephen Jay Gould, as quoted by Alister Mc-
Grath, "We neither affirm nor deny it; we simply can't comment
on it as scientists"—he indignantly responds, "Why shouldn't
we comment on God, as scientists?"[2] And if he is willing at
least to entertain the possibility that there might be a question
beyond the reach of science, it is only to affirm his confidence
that any such question must be beyond the reach of anyone
else, not least theologians, as well:

> Why are scientists so cravenly respectful towards the ambitions
> of theologians, over questions that theologians are certainly
> no more qualified to answer than scientists themselves? . . . If
> science cannot answer some ultimate question, what makes
> anybody think that religion can?[3]

Thus, for Dawkins, to believe in God is to hold to a scientific
hypothesis for which there is in fact no good evidence. Belief in
God is incapable of leading to insights or discoveries that regular
science cannot produce, and therefore should be abandoned.

It is important to note the nature of belief in this account:
belief is wholly, or at least fundamentally, a matter of intellectual assent based on evidence, and belief in God is intellectual
assent to a thoroughly dubious hypothesis. This construal is
reminiscent of Bertrand Russell's famous epigram that, if he
were confronted by God on the day of judgment and asked why
he had not believed in Him, he would respond, "Not enough
evidence, God, not enough evidence."[4] Belief in God, apparently, is like so much else in the world, in which acceptance
of a proposal depends on the strength of the evidence in its
favor. From a Christian perspective, it is not, of course, that

2. Dawkins, *God Delusion*, 55.
3. Dawkins, *God Delusion*, 56.
4. Russell's words are quoted approvingly by Dawkins in a "You Ask the Questions" feature in *The Independent*, December 4, 2006, http://www.independent.co.uk
/news/people/profiles/richard-dawkins-you-ask-the-questions-special-427003.html.

belief in God has nothing to do with evidence and reasons—far from it! But in setting up the whole issue in this particular way, Dawkins shows himself to be, like Russell, a true child of the classic seventeenth- and eighteenth-century Enlightenment account of religious belief, and correspondingly innocent of the ways in which the debates have moved on and issues have been reformulated and reconceptualized.[5]

> Over against this evidentialist mind-set, the issue is nicely reframed by Andrew Klavan: "God is not susceptible to proofs and disproofs. If you believe, the evidence is all around you. If you don't believe, no evidence can be enough."[6] Klavan's formulation has strong resonance with classic Christian theology and spirituality. For example, in the fourth century, St. Ephrem, who articulated his theological vision in poetry, wrote: "Lord, your symbols are everywhere, / yet you are hidden from everywhere" (*Hymns on Faith* 4.9).[7]

For Dawkins, as for Russell, faith (should it be warranted) would have to be based upon good evidence (should it exist), an understanding of which would appropriately lead to belief. Although it is not identical, this general stance has a certain real affinity to an "evidentialist" approach to the Bible, as briefly outlined at the beginning of this book: show that the Bible is reliable (i.e., historically accurate) where it can be tested, and on that basis trust it where it cannot be tested (i.e., in matters of faith and God). That this makes sense and can have value I

5. For a brief discussion of the history of ideas within which Dawkins stands, and an indication of why such ideas need revising, see excursus 3 following this chapter. Like the other excursuses in this book, it is in effect a lengthy small-type section that is not necessary for following my argument but may be of interest to those who want to understand more about, as one might perhaps put it, the transition of theological and philosophical thought from modernity to postmodernity.

6. Klavan, *Great Good Thing*, xxv.

7. The quotation is taken from a fine recent discussion of Ephrem's outlook, Sebastian Brock's "The Guidance of St. Ephrem: A Vision to Live By," in *The Practice of the Presence of God: Theology as a Way of Life*, ed. Martin Laird and Sheelah Treflé Hidden (London and New York: Routledge, 2017), 111.

do not wish to deny. But whether it is the best way of thinking about the Bible and its trustworthiness is another matter. I argued in chapter 3 that the significant initial evidence in relation to faith and the Bible may have more to do with the quality of certain people's lives and actions than with a persuasive argument that, say, John's Gospel shows a good, historically accurate knowledge of the city of Jerusalem in the time of Jesus and that Jesus' very own words might still be discerned within their Johannine phraseology.

For any evidentialist approach, the classic notion of theology as "faith seeking understanding" is likely to be a strange one. At best, it sounds like putting the cart before the horse ("Surely you should understand what faith is based on *before* you decide to believe"). At worst, it may amount to no more than irrational credulity seeking rationalization ("I don't want to look crazy in this stance I've taken and these claims I've made, so I'd better find some good-sounding things to back me up").[8] I propose, therefore, to look briefly at one of the key biblical passages that underlies the classic notion of faith seeking understanding. The passage is illuminating both for the nature of belief and for the nature of religious understanding in a biblical and Christian frame of reference.

Belief and Understanding in John 7:16–17[9]

The passage in question comes in the context of the ministry of Jesus in Jerusalem in John's Gospel. The narrative presents Jesus as teaching in the Jerusalem temple during the late-summer Feast of Booths/Tabernacles. Jesus' practice of

8. For a compelling account of what "faith seeking understanding" really means, see Nicholas Lash, "Anselm Seeking," in *The Beginning and the End of 'Religion'* (Cambridge: Cambridge University Press, 1995), 150–63.

9. In this section I develop material from my essay "How Can We Know the Truth? A Study of John 7:14–18," in *The Art of Reading Scripture*, ed. Ellen F. Davis and Richard B. Hays (Grand Rapids: Eerdmans, 2003), 239–57.

teaching in this setting is questioned by some on the grounds of his having "never been taught"; this may express straight-forward surprise at Jesus' ability to engage in learned disputa-tion without having undertaken formal training, though it might perhaps have more edge and be querying Jesus' credentials for public teaching. Either way, for present purposes my interest is in what Jesus says in response:

> [14]About the middle of the festival Jesus went up into the temple and began to teach. [15]The Jews were astonished at it, saying, "How does this man have such learning, when he has never been taught?" [16]Then Jesus answered them, "My teaching is not mine but his who sent me. [17]Anyone who resolves to do the will of God will know whether the teaching is from God or whether I am speaking on my own ["from myself," Greek *ap' emautou*]. [18]Those who speak on their own seek their own glory; but the one who seeks the glory of him who sent him is true, and there is nothing false in him." (John 7:14–18)

The issues raised here are as important and demanding as they come. If the claim is made, as Jesus here makes in verse 16, that his human words have their origin in God and do not merely originate from himself (as a self-serving expression of the desire for recognition from others), how can one really know that this is so? That is, how can one *test* it? Claims to speak for God are easily made, as history amply attests. But if such claims are unverifiable, if there is no way of determining whether God really is involved, then are they not ultimately meaningless, or else the expression of purely human priorities in a coded form? Indeed, should they not be considered potentially manipulative, an attempt to gain some kind of authority over others—either to get their admiration, or else to get them to do something that the speaker wants them to do but might not be able to get them to do otherwise? Although an appeal to God implies that the issue is one of ultimate right or truth, might the reality be no more than a disguised or coded human bid for one person/group to take control over another person/group?

Jesus says that there is a test of his claim that his teaching is from God. A preliminary ground-clearing point may help avoid misreading his words. To take the rhetorical idiom of the text seriously—Jesus' words that his teaching is "not mine but his who sent me"—entails not handling the text woodenly. Jesus is not inviting his hearers to imagine him to be a kind of ventriloquist's dummy, uttering words for God that intrinsically have nothing to do with him. In other words, he is not denying that his words are in a real sense the expression of his own heart and mind. But he is affirming that the *origin* of what is his is, in reality, God. This is made clear by the wording of 7:17: "whether . . . from God or . . . from myself."[10] In analytical rather than rhetorical terms, the force of Jesus' "not . . . but" in 7:16 is "not only . . . but also."[11]

The implicit, underlying claim that Jesus is making is that he is so open and responsive to God as his Father—that he is, as it were, so transparent to God ("Whoever has seen me has seen the Father," John 14:9)—that in his human words the word and will of God are accessible. Thus, in response to the question in 7:15 about how he could know what he knows without having done appropriate study, Jesus transposes the issue of theological insight from a matter of formal learning into the issue of responsiveness to God.

Thus the question is: How, if at all, might one be able in principle appropriately to recognize human words as not merely human but also as in some way authentically from God? Although the issue is raised here specifically with regard to the

10. The NRSV rendering, "on my own," loses something of the text's contrast between "from God" and "from myself."

11. For comparable Pauline usage of this idiom, see Gal. 2:20; 1 Cor. 15:10. A striking Old Testament example is Deut. 5:3.

teaching of Jesus as portrayed by John, it is also one that is raised, in one way or another, by the Christian understanding that the Bible's human words are "the lively oracles of God." It is unsurprising, therefore, that Christian theologians through the ages have tended to generalize the crux of this particular Johannine passage into a principle of wide applicability.

Some readers may wonder about the status of words on the lips of Jesus in John's distinctive portrayal, in which Jesus speaks in a manner so different from his characteristic forms of speech in the Synoptic Gospels. Put differently: there are well-known questions about the relationship between "the world within the text" (what Jesus says here) and "the world behind the text" (the nature of the "historical Jesus" and the role of the author and the "Johannine community"). For the present, I would just say briefly that the Jesus who is authoritative for Christian faith is Jesus *as interpreted by the evangelists*. The issue is not whether the evangelists have interpreted Jesus (they have), or whether John's interpretation is peculiarly distinctive (it is), but whether these interpretations are *reliable*—indeed, *true*—interpretations of the significance of Jesus' life, teaching, death, and resurrection. The question of appropriate criteria for evaluating such a claim (not an easy question!) will emerge to some extent in my wider discussion. But part of the meaning of the church's making John a canonical Gospel—that is, an authoritative part of Scripture—is precisely that this portrayal, this interpretation, of Jesus is to be trusted in terms of faith and life. The testimony of many Christians through the ages, including some of its most eminent theologians, is that they have found John's Gospel to be where, as it were, the heartbeat of Jesus can be heard, as when the beloved disciple, the implied author of the Gospel (John 21:24), reclines so close to Jesus that he could be said to be "on Jesus' chest" (13:23, 25; NRSV's "next to him" weakens the Greek idiom)—just as Jesus himself is the one who, as the Word, is "close to the Father's heart" (1:18, with the same Greek idiom "on the chest" as in 13:23, 25).

The criterion for grasping that the true origin of Jesus' words is God is clear: it is that one must resolve to do the will of God.[12] What does this mean? The primary cross-reference within the

---

12. The NRSV loses the way in which the Greek repeats the root *thelō* as both verb and noun: "be willing to do His will."

Gospel is Jesus' response to the crowds in the previous chapter. When they ask, "What must we do to perform the works of God?," Jesus responds, "This is the work of God, that you believe in him whom he has sent" (John 6:28–29). The general question about "the works"[13] God requires is given a specific answer. There is one thing to do—that is, to believe / have faith in Jesus; this, in the famous Lukan wording (Luke 10:42), is "the one thing needful." Although it is common to contrast a Johannine sense of doing God's will as *belief* with a Synoptic sense of doing God's will as *moral action* (e.g., Matt. 7:21–23)— and there is undoubtedly some real difference between the two portrayals—it would be unwise to draw any sharp contrast. For the Johannine sense of "believing" is a responsive focusing of the whole person on Jesus. This responsiveness includes a clear cognitive dimension ("believe that Jesus is the Messiah/Christ, the Son of God," John 20:31), but is also concerned with the totality of how a person lives. When Jesus says elsewhere that he is "the way" to the Father, he is letting his disciples know that the way in which he lives in relation to the Father is the way in which they too must live if they are to come to the Father (14:3–6); and Jesus says that "the one who believes in me will also do the works that I do" (14:12), because belief in Jesus means becoming like him in what one does, or seeks to do.

Thus the key point is that a certain kind of knowledge— that particular human words genuinely originate with God—is inseparable from a certain kind of personal responsiveness. The knowledge that is envisaged is participatory. Unless heart and mind have a certain openness towards that which Jesus says and does, the issue of divine origin can only be a matter of mere words, a contestable and unverifiable claim. Whether faith comes in a flash or is a slow and possibly hesitant process

13. *Ta erga*, i.e., actions, not least the kinds of thing that a person would normally do to acquire food for life, which is the subject in context.

does not affect the point that without at least some degree of participatory faith, any possible divine reality in Jesus remains beyond human perception. There is an empirical dimension to faith, but it is the empiricism not of the natural sciences but of the existential engagement of a person with dimensions of reality that can easily remain opaque to the unresponsive.

In the context of my wider argument, this dimension of personal faith and engagement is a necessary corollary to the persuasive force of a Christian plausibility structure. The plausibility of significant others should not just lead one to become a member of an attractive group as an end in itself, though of course this may happen. Rather, one should be led on to dare to believe that which these others believe, that in and through the biblical portrayal of the person, teaching, and works of Jesus (in his life, death, and resurrection) the reality of the living God is encountered. One's trust in people can and should lead to trust in the book they trust, which in turn can and should lead to trust in the reality of God, supremely in the person of Jesus, that this book conveys. This creates a constant feedback system in which, at least in principle (though in practice there can often be difficulties and complications), trust in God through Jesus leads to trust in the biblical documents, and one's initial trust is confirmed and deepened. At every stage, existential engagement through deciding to place one's trust here, and not somewhere else, is indispensable to making progress.

It should also be said that such trust should not shut down critical awareness of possible problems along the way, either in relation to the people in the plausibility structure, or to the book that portrays Jesus and the ways of God, or even to what trust in God does and does not mean. It may well be that learning to hold together both trust and critical awareness—standing back within that trust so as to try to appraise facets of what it should and should not entail—takes time; but that is life. Trust is not naïveté or a shutting of one's eyes to awkward facts, but rather constitutes an enabling context within which difficulties may be recognized and responsibly handled. (Admittedly, difficulties can sometimes overwhelm trust, and faith may be abandoned. But that is essentially to recognize that disasters can strike.)

I am thus arguing for two key elements in relation to coming to have faith in God through the content of the Bible. First, there needs to be an openness to taking the Bible seriously as a key to making sense of the world, an openness that is usually best fostered through the persuasive impact of the life and thought of other Christians, both past and present. This openness is focused in the recognition of the biblical documents as canonical—that is, the Christian privileging of these particular writings—which creates expectations that the deity of whom they speak is the true God, and that the faith of which they speak is still a viable option today. Second, there needs to be an existential engagement, a responsive openness to the God whom Jesus represents, as the only way in which words relating to God can cease to be just words *about* God but can also become words *from* God that convey a living divine reality.

The Case Study: *Aeneid* 1, Daniel 7, and Matthew 28

At this stage we must return to our case study, the comparison and evaluation of the visions of a sovereign deity bequeathing unending dominion to a particular people in *Aeneid* 1 and Daniel 7.

A Modern Christian Reading of Virgil and "Limitless Empire"

Although historic and contemporary readings of Virgil are almost limitless, I want briefly to consider one modern Christian interpretation, that of T. S. Eliot (1888–1965), from around the middle of the twentieth century (though for reasons of space it will be necessary to ignore Eliot's wider discussions from which my extracts are taken).[14]

Eliot is happy to privilege Virgil as a distinctive and supreme author who stands in a unique relation to European civilization: "Virgil . . . is at the centre of European civilization, in a position which no other poet can share or usurp. The Roman Empire and the Latin language were not any empire and any language, but an empire and language with a unique destiny in relation to ourselves."[15] In an essay entitled "Virgil and the Christian World," Eliot sees Virgil as a pivotal figure "at the end of the pre-Christian and at the beginning of the Christian world. He looks both ways; he makes a liaison between the old world and the new."[16] Indeed, Eliot makes an intriguing claim:

> Virgil made of Roman civilization in his poetry something better than it really was. His sensibility is more nearly Christian than that of any other Greek or Roman poet: not like that of an early Christian perhaps, but like that of Christianity from the time at which we can say that a Christian civilization had come into being.[17]

In general terms, he says this of the vision of empire in the *Aeneid*:

> There, Virgil is concerned with the *imperium romanum*, with the extension and justification of imperial rule. He sets an ideal

14. For a cultural contextualization of Eliot's approach to Virgil, see Theodore Ziolkowski, *Virgil and the Moderns* (Princeton: Princeton University Press, 1993), 99–145.

15. T. S. Eliot, "What Is a Classic?" (1944), in *On Poetry and Poets* (London: Faber & Faber, 1957), 68.

16. Eliot, "Virgil and the Christian World" (1951), in *On Poetry and Poets*, 123.

17. Eliot, "Virgil and the Christian World," 125.

for Rome, and for empire in general, which was never realized in history; but the ideal of empire as Virgil sees it is a noble one.

Eliot then cites Jupiter's famous lines about limitless empire (*Aen.* 1.278–79), together with those of Anchises about bringing peace, sparing the conquered, and striking down the haughty (6.851–53), and comments thus:

> I say that it was all the end of history that Virgil could be asked to find, and that it was a worthy end. And do you really think that Virgil was mistaken? You must remember that the Roman Empire was transformed into the Holy Roman Empire. What Virgil proposed to his contemporaries was the highest ideal even for an unholy Roman Empire, for any merely temporal empire. We are all, so far as we inherit the civilization of Europe, still citizens of the Roman Empire, and time has not yet proved Virgil wrong when he wrote *nec tempora pono: imperium sine fine dedi* [i.e., Jupiter's "For them I will not limit time. . . . Their rule will have no end"]. But, of course, the Roman Empire which Virgil imagined and for which Aeneas worked out his destiny was not exactly the same as the Roman Empire of the legionaries, the pro-consuls and governors, the business men and speculators, the demagogues and generals. It was something greater, but something which exists because Virgil imagined it. It remains an ideal, but one which Virgil passed on to Christianity to develop and to cherish.[18]

In a contemporary culture where postcolonial suspicion of empires is widespread, it may not be easy to hear Eliot. He is one of the last witnesses to the enormous hold that the Roman Empire, as represented by Virgil and in one way or another appropriated by Christianity, had on the European mind for most of Europe's history. Eliot is trying to articulate a moral

18. Eliot, "Virgil and the Christian World," 129–30.

vision of the world as expressed by Virgil and to resist a reductive reading of this vision. He is not interested in the status of Jupiter or Roman religion, but he is interested in the portrayals of destiny and duty that he sees in the *Aeneid*. He reads Virgil not so much in relation to the time of Augustus and the possible legitimation of a new political order under Augustus—though he is well aware of that dimension of the text—as in relation to a moral vision that has an intrinsic integrity above and beyond the situation in which it arose, an ideal that critiques a merely military and mercenary vision of empire. This vision was congenial within a Christian frame of reference and thereby contributed to the historic civilization of Europe. As someone who in his adult life had lived through the two European wars that became world wars, Eliot knew the depths to which European civilization could sink. And yet he holds to the value and importance of a classic moral vision that shows a better way.

The richness of Virgil's moral vision is well known, not least through famous lines such as "the world is a world of tears and the burdens of mortality touch the heart" (*sunt lacrimae rerum et mentem mortalia tangunt, Aen.* 1.462).[19] One interesting example—perhaps the kind of thing that Eliot envisaged, though admittedly not an example he specified in these essays—can be seen in Virgil's portrayal of Aeneas. One of the primary responsibilities for Aeneas and his descendants is, in the words of his father, Anchises, to "spare the conquered" (*parcere subiectis*, 6.853). The *Aeneid* concludes with a battle between Aeneas and Turnus, his primary opponent. This combat ends with Aeneas standing over a defeated Turnus, who surrenders. Turnus is "conquered" (*subiectus*). Aeneas initially hesitates over what to do and is inclined to be merciful and spare (*parcere*) his opponent. But he suddenly notices on Turnus the belt of Pallas, Aeneas's companion who had previously been killed by Turnus. In a surge of grief and rage Aeneas invokes Pallas and kills Turnus. Virgil knows how easily a noble moral vision can be overcome by destructive human passions, without the vision being nullified thereby. However, like many a biblical (especially Old Testament) narrator, Virgil

19. The translation here, as in ch. 1, is from Fagles (*Aeneid* 1.558–59, p. 63, in translation).

tells a rich and demanding story without offering evaluative comment. The depth of his portrayal is one of many factors in his enduring appeal.

Eliot represents a Christian appropriation of Virgil's vision of Rome as transmuted into an enduring image of European culture, in which the *Aeneid* arguably comes as close to being a counterpart to Christian Scripture as perhaps any pagan classic ever could. Nonetheless, even if Eliot was right that "time has not yet proved Virgil wrong when he wrote *nec tempora pono: imperium sine fine dedi*" (though one wonders what Eliot would have allowed to count for making any such judgment), it is surely the case that this vision of "unending rule / limitless empire" for Rome and its legacy has finally lost its hold on the European imagination. For better or worse, it simply does not matter any longer in the way that it once did. And although the *Aeneid* remains a classic, its reading is increasingly confined to scholars, even though there clearly remains a public for new translations.

And so we return to one of my basic questions: If the Bible is not to go the same way as Virgil, and is to be more than interesting religious thought and/or a collection of memorable stories from the past, then on what basis is the case for it to be made? Before the various strands of my argument can be finally pulled together, one further element in the case study needs to be put in place: the relationship between Daniel 7 and the New Testament portrayal of Jesus.

Daniel 7 and Matthew 28: Jesus and Unlimited Authority

I would like to reframe the discussion of Daniel 7 by turning to another comparable passage, with a comparable vision: the well-known New Testament narrative of one of Jesus' resurrection appearances in Matthew 28:18–20.[20]

20. Analogously to my referring to parts of Jupiter's speech in book 1 of the *Aeneid* simply as *Aeneid* 1, I will refer to these few verses in Matthew 28 simply as "Matthew 28" (as already above in the section heading and subheading).

This is a passage in which it is particularly important that discussions about the possible world behind the text—in terms of tradition, redaction, and composition, or the life of the early church with its possible baptismal formulae and practices, not to mention doctrinal controversies—should not displace the discipline of taking the world within the text itself with full imaginative seriousness.

On a mountain in Galilee, the risen Jesus meets with his disciples. Although they are initially somewhat hesitant, and perhaps simply unsure of what to make of the risen Jesus, Jesus clarifies what his resurrection means:

> And Jesus came and said to them, "All authority [*pasa exousia*] in heaven and on earth has been given [*edothē*] to me. Go therefore and make disciples of all nations [*panta ta ethnē*], baptizing them in the name of the Father and of the Son and of the Holy Spirit, and teaching them to obey everything that I have commanded you. And remember, I am with you always, to the end of the age [*aiōn*]." (Matt. 28:18–20)

Although Jesus' words are fully meaningful in their own terms in the immediate narrative context, they also resonate strongly with the vision of the dominion that the Ancient One gives to the figure who appears as a human being in Daniel 7:14. Thus this resurrection appearance of Jesus is appropriately read in relation to—indeed, as a realization of—the Daniel vision.

The precise relationship between the narrative of Matthew 28 and the vision of Daniel 7 is open to debate, as the evangelist does not explicitly mention Daniel 7. However, the resonance of both language and content is strong. Matthew elsewhere tends to cite Israel's scriptures via their ancient Greek rendering, and the Septuagint renders the portrayal of the son of man / human being in Daniel 7:14 thus:

> And royal authority [*exousia*] was given [*edothē*] to him,
>   and all the nations [*panta ta ethnē*] of the earth according
>   to posterity,
>   and all honor was serving him.

And his authority [*exousia*] is an everlasting [*aiōnios*] authority,
which shall never be removed—
and his kingship [*basileia*], which will never perish.[21]

The common wording and content make it highly likely that Matthew's final portrayal of the risen Jesus envisages Jesus as embodying and fulfilling Daniel 7. Two chapters previously, in Matthew's portrayal of Jesus' trial before the high priest, Jesus explicitly cites the Daniel 7 vision—"But I tell you, from now on you will see the Son of Man seated at the right hand of Power and coming on the clouds of heaven" (Matt. 26:64, using the words of Dan. 7:13)—in a context where he is enduring faithfully while at the mercy of others who are behaving bestially. And not long before that, "the climactic passage of Jesus' teaching in Matthew, the great parable of the final judgment (Matt. 25:31–46), depicts 'all the nations [*panta ta ethnē*]' being gathered before the throne of the Son of Man—a transparent allusion to the scene of final enthronement in Daniel 7:13–14."[22] Apart from the likely deliberate allusion to Daniel 7 on the part of Matthew, this linkage can also be appropriately made on intertextual grounds, independent of authorial intention. The shared language and subject matter of the two passages, when they are both read as constituent parts of the Christian Bible, makes it natural to read the later passage in light of the earlier.

An unrestricted authority (*exousia*) for Jesus, not only on earth but also in heaven, is comparable in implication to the visions of empire and dominion of *Aeneid* 1 and Daniel 7. Previously we noted that "in each context a sovereign deity (Jupiter, the Ancient One) bestows sovereignty on earth (*imperium*, *sholtān*) upon a specially favored people (Romans, Jews), a sovereignty that explicitly has no envisaged termination but is to be endlessly enduring (*sine fine*, *'ad-'ālmā'*)."[23] Here too is a similar fourfold correspondence.

If Jesus has *all authority in heaven*, then Jesus fully and unreservedly speaks and acts for God. The risen Jesus shares

21. This is the rendering of the Old Greek in NETS (p. 1012). The textual problems of the relationship between the Old Greek and Theodotion make no real difference to the point at issue, and so can be passed over.

22. Richard B. Hays, *Echoes of Scripture in the Gospels* (Waco: Baylor University Press, 2016), 183.

23. Above, ch. 1, p. 34.

the status and majesty of the Ancient One and so is also comparable to Jupiter in dignity and role.

If Jesus has *all authority on earth*, then that authority in some way transcends that of regular authorities on earth, be it the emperor in Rome or any other king or ruler; all other authorities anywhere are in some way relativized by and subject to Jesus' authority. Thus the *exousia* on earth that Jesus has, in the light of which he commissions his disciples, is equivalent to the *imperium* that Jupiter gives and the *sholtān* that the Ancient One gives.

Jesus' commission to his disciples is comparable to the sovereign bequests to particular recipients in *Aeneid* 1 and Daniel 7. These particular disciples are the initial recipients and thereby conveyors of Jesus' authority. Thus Jesus' disciples—namely, Christians—are in a certain way equivalent to Romans and Jews as privileged recipients of the divine bequest.

Jesus' commission to his disciples is for the benefit of "all nations"—that is, any and every human community, without restriction.[24] People everywhere are to be brought into the reality of Jesus' authority and have a new identity, allegiance, and way of living that expresses that reality. Moreover, this commission is not meant to have a potentially limited span of time, but rather has no time limit, for what is envisaged will continue "until the end of the age/world." Thus Jesus' authoritative commission is equivalent in extent and duration to *sine fine* and *'ad 'ālmā'*.

The Nature and Content of Jesus' Authority in Matthew's Gospel

What is the nature and content of this universal authority of Jesus? In general terms, Matthew 28 clearly draws attention to

24. There is an interpretive question about whether the meaning of *panta ta ethnē* is "all nations" or, more restrictively, "all gentiles." Most commentators through the ages have opted for the unrestricted sense, a sense that is fully appropriate in context, and I see no reason to differ. The issue is fully discussed in Ulrich Luz, *Matthew 21–28*, Hermeneia (Minneapolis: Fortress, 2005), 628–31.

the practice of baptism—that is, people making a fresh start and entering into the newly understood divine reality of God as Father, Son, and Holy Spirit. There is also a clear note of obedience to Jesus' teaching, teaching that is extensively presented in the preceding pages of the Gospel. Making disciples envisages people adopting practices of discipleship (so there is here, in Dietrich Bonhoeffer's well-known words from *The Cost of Discipleship*, no "cheap grace").

Beyond this, the nature of the authority of which Jesus speaks is given content by Matthew's overall portrayal of the person of Jesus.[25] For this final scene of the Gospel resonates strongly with a scene at the very outset of Jesus' ministry, immediately after his baptism. When Jesus is tested/tempted in the desert, the third of his temptations takes this form:

> Again, the devil took him to a very high mountain and showed him all the kingdoms of the world and their splendor; and he said to him, "All these I will give you, if you will fall down and worship me." Jesus said to him, "Away with you, Satan! for it is written, 'Worship the Lord your God, and serve only him.'"
> (Matt. 4:8–10)

In both Matthew 4 and Matthew 28, Jesus is situated on a mountain (*oros*), and the issue spoken about is that of ultimate sovereignty (*exousia*)[26] in relation to Jesus as divine son (*huios*), and possible submission (*proskynēsis*). The sovereignty that Jesus declines to take at the beginning of his ministry (Matt. 4) is given to him by God after his resurrection (Matt. 28). This

25. In this present account I draw on my earlier and fuller discussion in *The Bible, Theology, and Faith: A Study of Abraham and Jesus*, CSCD (Cambridge: Cambridge University Press, 2000), ch. 6.

26. Surprisingly, the wording of Matt. 4:8–9 does not contain the word *exousia* ("authority"), even though it is present in the parallel account in Luke 4:6 and could have been in the evangelists' putative *Vorlage* (Q). Nonetheless, the conceptual linkage remains clear.

framing, then, suggests a particular question in reading the Gospel: How must Jesus as Son of God live, what must he do, so that at the end of his time on earth, God *gives* him the sovereignty that he refuses at the outset to *take*? The nature, content, and meaning of his sovereignty is surely determined by this.

In the temptation in the wilderness, the question of what it means for Jesus to be Son of God, as just pronounced by the heavenly voice at his baptism (Matt. 3:17), is probed. The first two temptations explicitly begin with "If you are the Son of God . . ." (4:3, 6), and all three temptations revolve around whether Jesus will use divine power for his own benefit. Each time, Jesus declines and finds the meaning of his sonship in scriptural portrayals of responsive obedience to God.

At a key turning point in Jesus' ministry, at Caesarea Philippi, Peter recognizes Jesus as "the Messiah/Christ, the Son of the living God" (Matt. 16:16), and the rest of that episode revolves around the meaning of this identity and vocation. When Jesus interprets his vocation in terms of suffering, dying, and being raised, and Peter remonstrates with him, Jesus rebukes Peter with "Get behind me, Satan!" (16:23)—the same words with which he rejects the third temptation in the wilderness (4:10).[27] Jesus recognizes that Peter's words represent a renewal of the temptation in the wilderness, a proposal to implement his special vocation in a way that would diminish the cost of his obedience and thereby attempt to make it easier for him.

Not only at the outset and in the middle of his ministry is the meaning of Jesus' vocation as Son of God probed. At the end, as Jesus hangs dying on the cross, passersby scornfully call out, "You who would destroy the temple and build it in

27. It appears that the most likely original wording of Matt. 4:10 is *hypage satana* ("Get back, Satan"), while in 16:23 it is *hypage opisō mou satana* ("Get back behind me, Satan"). But the large number of manuscripts that also have *opisō mou* ("behind me") in 4:10 is evidence that ancient copyists regularly linked the two passages, an interpretive linkage that encouraged a textual conflation.

three days [i.e., you who claim to have special divine power], save yourself! If you are the Son of God, come down from the cross" (Matt. 27:40). *If you are the Son of God.* It is no longer just a matter of Jesus easing his hunger by turning stones into bread, but rather of saving himself from an agonizing death: What's the point in having special power if you don't use it for yourself when it really counts? If you don't use it, perhaps you don't really have it. Religious leaders similarly mock Jesus' messianic role: "He is the King of Israel; let him come down from the cross now, and we will believe in him" (27:42). If Jesus is a David or one greater than David, then he should demonstrate it by saving himself from death. Indeed, he can fulfill his mission to Israel by so doing, for they, the accredited leaders of Israel, will then believe in him. His mission can be accomplished here and now—it is only a moment away. It is the final temptation. But those who want to see Jesus' divine power at work see only Jesus remaining on the cross, crying out in an agony of dereliction (misunderstood as a cry for help) and dying.

Matthew of course makes clear that there was more going on in the death of Jesus than met the eye of his mockers, for he recounts an astonishing sequence of earthshaking and life-bestowing events that show to the policeman on duty, and one or two others, the nature and meaning of Jesus as God's Son (Matt. 27:51–54). Nonetheless, to most of those present at the crucifixion, Jesus appeared to be a failure.

It is the Jesus who lives and dies thus—who consistently refuses to use divine power to make things easier for himself or to save himself—who is raised from the tomb and appears to his disciples on a mountain in Galilee, saying, "All authority in heaven and on earth has been given to me." That which he refused to take has been given to him. How and why? Because of the way in which he understood and lived out his earthly vocation as Son of God, with a costly and obedient trust in his Father and concern for others that took precedence over all concern to further his own well-being. The fact that Jesus does not use his sonship to his own advantage but rather is willing to undergo suffering and death while being mocked and misunderstood, and yet then is raised from death to receive sovereign and universal authority, gives meaning to this authority. When the risen Jesus commissions his disciples, the disciples are reassured that, in fulfilling this commission, they will not be on their own, but in some way will be accompanied by the very one in whose authority they act. In other words, the way in which they fulfill their commission needs to embody and represent that reality and authority of the risen Jesus into which they also bring others.

This narrative movement in Matthew's Gospel—Jesus declines to realize what it means to be Son of God in terms of his own self-advantage, and he declines to take sovereign authority but in his resurrection receives it—almost irresistibly calls to mind one of the most famous passages in the Letters of Paul. In Philippians 2, Paul memorably depicts Christ Jesus as one who,

> though he was in the form of God,
>   did not regard equality with God
>   as something to be exploited,
> but emptied himself,
>   taking the form of a slave,
>   being born in human likeness.
> And being found in human form,
>   he humbled himself
>   and became obedient to the point of death—
>   even death on a cross.
> Therefore God also highly exalted him
>   and gave him the name
>   that is above every name,
> so that at the name of Jesus
>   every knee should bend,
>   in heaven and on earth and under the earth,

and every tongue should confess
   that Jesus Christ is Lord,
   to the glory of God the Father. (Phil. 2:6–11)

The one who would not exploit his divine prerogative receives a sovereign accolade; the one who humbles himself to a cruel death is given life and is eternally exalted.

On Understanding Jesus' Authority

How should this universal authority of Jesus in both Matthew and Paul be understood? It is in fact not easy to find good categories to depict it. It involves unreserved trust in and obedience towards God. There is a particular human face to the authority of God, for Jesus represents and constitutes that authority. There is a recognition that the outworking of God's authority on earth is far from straightforward. There is an important sense in which Jesus' authority is a "moral" and "spiritual" authority—the sovereignty, the ultimate supremacy, of a certain kind of faithfulness and goodness and justice, even in the face of evil, suffering, and death. Yet such categories need careful handling, not least because of pervasive tendencies in contemporary culture to construe "spiritual" as the opposite of "material," and "moral" as (often though not always) "idealistic"; these construals can reduce the moral and spiritual to things that one might hope for privately but that make little difference to everyday social, political, and economic life, in which other "realities" pertain and constrain. But the concern of Matthew's narrative, as of Paul's account, is to depict something that is already true about the world here and now: that Jesus has a sovereignty that transcends, and thereby relativizes, all other authorities. It is a message for all, for it represents a definitive reality about our world, a reality that is not theoretical, not only because of its practical realization by Jesus but also because his disciples from his day until now are called to bear witness to it. Insofar as these Christian disciples, as human groups, necessarily have social, political, and economic dimensions to their existence, their vocation is in one way or another to constitute a public, social embodiment of that of which Jesus speaks—though the nature of the social reality that Christian people, the body of Christ, are meant to be is always an open and continuously negotiable issue.

One facet of Jesus' authority can be seen from the way in which the Gospels portray Jesus' earthly ministry—and the authority that he already had and implemented in that context—in terms of the ease with which it was liable to misunderstanding. Not only was it noncoercive (the rich young man responded to Jesus' challenge by going away [Matt. 19:16–22//Mark 10:17–22//Luke 18:18–23]), but it was also easily misrepresented (as at Jesus' trial and crucifixion). This is no less true of his authority after he is raised from death. We should remember that in no Gospel portrayal does the risen Jesus ever confront those who were responsible for his death with the error of their ways, as though the truth of his resurrection could be presented as something incontrovertible that straightforwardly overturns wrong understandings—for example, "Look at me, Caiaphas. See how utterly mistaken you were! Here I am, Pilate. See how blind and wrong you were!" This means that Jesus' resurrection is a reality that is likely to be recognizable only by, and make sense only to, a certain kind of openness and trust—to a conscience that will recognize the risen Jesus as representing sovereign goodness, rightness, and truth. If Jesus' life, both earthly and risen, represents an ultimate truth about God and the world, it is a truth that is not self-evident and that may become evident only in the context of a certain kind of responsiveness to it.

To put this in terms of my wider thesis: faith—that is, positive response to God through Jesus in relation to the content of the Bible—will always be much more than inferences from evidence and arguments. The firm "evidence" that a Russell or a Dawkins requires is not on offer, because it is not what is really needed to bring the reality of God alive in the human heart and mind.

How, then, should our two biblical passages about divine authority being bestowed on humans, Daniel 7 and Matthew 28, be understood in relation to each other? Although it was important initially to attend to Daniel 7 on its own terms, as a pre-Christian vision with its own integrity, its Christian understanding should surely not be separated from its Christian counterpart in Matthew 28. Christians preserve Daniel 7 as part of a two-testament Bible that is greater than, and can give fuller meaning to, its individual parts. That is to say, whatever might be envisaged by the vision of Daniel 7 both in itself and in the broader canonical context of Israel's scriptures, its Christian realization should not be considered to be other than, or separate from, the realization of Matthew 28. In other words, from a Christian perspective there are not two distinct sovereign dominions bequeathed by divine authority, but one.

Daniel 7 itself is unspecific about the form to be taken by the properly human dominion that replaces that of the bestial kings, but within the Christian canon Jesus is the human figure ("the son of man") who embodies the realization of that dominion. Many aspects of Daniel 7 still straightforwardly pertain to this Christian context. For example, the implied qualities of faithfulness, endurance, and wise understanding in the here and now that characterize the recipients of the divine bequest in Daniel 7 do not cease to apply to the disciples—both the first ones and those who come after them—who receive Jesus' bequest in Matthew 28. And importantly, Daniel's vision of Israel vindicated and exercising authority over other nations is now realized and enacted through the disciples' mission to make disciples of all nations. In *this* way, divine authority will be implemented in the world ("on earth, as it is in heaven"). As Richard Hays puts it, "Integral to Matthew's vision . . . is his insistence that the sovereignty of God over the nations will become effectual through nonviolent means. The nations are 'conquered,' as it were, through baptism into the name of the Father and of the Son and of the Holy Spirit and through their instruction to obey the teachings of a master who has insisted that the meaning of the Torah is summed up in acts of love and mercy."[28]

> The question of the roles of the world's various faiths and traditions, both religious and other, within this sovereignty of Christ needs separate discussion. I hope it will be clear from what has been said, however, that the nature of the Christian vision is not "imperialist," other than in terms of the sovereignty of divine justice, mercy, and goodness as realized in Jesus, and the necessity of faithful human witness to this. It is undeniable, however, that through the ages this vision has all too easily and frequently been co-opted into imperialist projects that have been expressed in other terms.

Aeneid 1, Daniel 7, and Matthew 28: Criteria for Privileging the Biblical Accounts

It is time now to return to the questions at the heart of the case-study discussion. How should the vision of Daniel 7 be understood if read alongside the vision of *Aeneid* 1? Is there any good reason that the vision of Daniel 7 should not be seen as essentially similar to the vision of *Aeneid* 1—that is, as a fascinating part of the history of the human mind and human society, but one with no continuing truth value in the world of today? How and why might one read and evaluate Daniel 7 differently from *Aeneid* 1? On what basis, if any, might one recognize the one true God in the Ancient One of Daniel 7 but not in the Jupiter of *Aeneid* 1?

28. Hays, *Echoes of Scripture in the Gospels*, 184–85.

I will draw on the preceding discussion to try to formulate at least preliminary answers to these questions.

Belief in God as Integrally Linked to the Persistence of Plausibility Structures

A first key factor is the social nature of belief and knowledge, both in the ancient world and today, as set out in chapter 3. Questions about belief in the deities depicted in *Aeneid* 1 and Daniel 7 should not be posed in the abstract, as though they could be responsibly answered apart from attention to the continuity (or otherwise) of a community that privileges a document and its content. Although *Aeneid* 1 was long privileged by Roman culture and its successors—and the wider vision of the *Aeneid* could still be privileged by Eliot in the mid-twentieth century—its deity, Jupiter, has almost no advocates today.[29] Almost no one today regards ancient Roman religion, or Jupiter, as a live option, even though of course important elements of Stoicism and Epicureanism have survived in other forms. By contrast, the deity of Daniel 7, understood as the God of Abraham and Israel, has had substantial communities of believers—initially solely Jewish but soon also Christian—continuously throughout history. The church functions as a plausibility structure not only through its contemporary witness but also through its persistence through the centuries in maintaining the importance of a particular way of seeing God, the world, and ourselves.

Now of course mere persistence through time is no guarantee of value or truth, as any reflection on the phenomenon of astrology quickly indicates. Error and folly may be stubbornly long-lived and liable to revival just when one thought

29. An absolute denial that worshipers of Jupiter exist, such as that of H. L. Mencken (above, p. 28), now has to be qualified just a little by the rise of a neo-paganism movement in Greece that looks to ancient Greek deities (e.g., Jupiter as Zeus).

(and hoped) that they had died. Dawkins notes that the God of Abraham still has adherents today in a way that other ancient deities do not, but sees this only as an annoying aberration, an inconsistent exception that (he hopes) will soon cease to be the case.[30] He and others would say that it is the understanding of the world attained through the natural and social sciences that will at last liberate us from previous, mistaken understandings of the world, as in the Bible.

Nonetheless, even if the persistence of biblically oriented faith through time is not a sufficient condition of its possible truthfulness, it remains a necessary condition. For the continuing existence of the Jewish and Christian faiths constitutes a certain kind of plausibility structure that generates assumptions and expectations about their sacred texts, which are held to be authoritative, and that seeks to embody those texts' content. These assumptions and expectations are paradigmatically displayed in contexts of worship, where the reading and exposition of Scripture, and singing and prayer that use its language, shape believers on a regular basis. We assume and expect, because countless others have assumed and expected before us and have found these assumptions and expectations to be fruitful. Thus, questions about privileging the portrayal of the deity and the human-like figure in Daniel 7 are inseparable from the evaluation of those continuing patterns of life and thought that are a constituent part of that privileging: Who, for people today, are the significant others whose perspectives are considered desirable? However much one can in principle distinguish these issues and break them down analytically, and differentiate between the singers and the song, the point is that appropriate evaluation of a song about God must take the believing singers into account as part of a responsible overall understanding.

30. See above, ch. 1, p. 28.

Learning over Time and Developing in Understanding

A second factor in answering the questions posed above relates to the importance of taking seriously what has been learned, especially in modernity, about the nature of history and historical development. This has some similarities to, though is distinct from, the importance of appropriate historical-critical awareness in the reading of the Bible that I have maintained throughout.

The persistence of a plausibility structure through time brings with it other implications, implications that often tend, not always helpfully, to be depicted as the "development of doctrine." The significant point is that both thought and practice develop and are modified over time as circumstances of life change; recognizing this is a necessary element in contemporary belief in ancient biblical content. Of course, there are difficult questions about when a development constitutes a genuine deepening and/or refinement, and when it might constitute a poor appropriation and/or corruption. For present purposes, the point is that the Christian church, from earliest times, has sought to clarify, refine, and deepen its belief in God and has hosted extensive and searching debates about what it does and does not mean to have true belief in God. Judaism through the ages also has, in its own way, comparably probed, refined, and reconstrued the biblical content even as it has appropriated it. The differing ways in which we understand and live in the world through our knowledge gained from the natural and social sciences also make a huge difference to the context in which we seek to understand and use the Bible.

Put differently: the existence of a plausibility structure does not mean that one can deny or dismiss, even while one may sometimes temporarily postpone, questions of appropriate conceptual rigor and coherence and their corresponding moral and existential implications. My argument is not that people today should somehow try to recapture the mind-set and worldview of ancient Jews (even if not of Romans) around the turn of the eras, as though knowledge that has emerged through the centuries could simply be set aside. Rather, my argument is that belief in the deity of Daniel 7 is meaningful only when it is mediated through the broader context of the canonical scriptures of ancient Israel. This belief is itself meaningful for Christians only when it is mediated and appropriated through Jesus and the New Testament, and when the whole Christian canon is mediated through ongoing theological debates and practices of life and worship. These debates and practices in turn refine and clarify such belief in terms of what it should and should not entail. Thereby, contemporary rules of faith and life are articulated. Of course, Christian beliefs grow out of and stand in continuity with the faith of Israel in the Old Testament, and that ancient faith remains in certain ways normative. However, my concern is not to repristinate an ancient mind-set, but rather to understand how both the persistence and the development of that ancient faith in its Christian frame of reference make it possible for believers today to enter into a belief in God that is not identical to, but does stand in real continuity with, that of ancient Israel.

The Nature of Revelation

A third factor is the question of what "revelation" does and does not mean. If God has, as it were, faded from the picture in the modern world, and the study of the human dimensions of the Bible has become an end in itself—with a tendency to see what the biblical writers say about God solely as human constructions, items in the history of religious and ideological thought—how might progress be made beyond this apparent impasse?

There are at least two endemic problems in much modern thought about God. On the one hand, the notion of revelation is often understood in a "trump card" kind of way. Believers can be thought to have access to knowledge "from beyond"—perhaps a vision of the divine, as in Daniel 7—that is thereby considered immune to critique. This can then be contrasted with the paradigm of knowledge in the modern world. Here knowledge is empirically derived, can be tested in practice, and is thereby open to correction as and when necessary, reflecting a process of genuine learning to know and understand, unlike the rigid and unchallengeable way of dogmatic claims and impositions.

On the other hand, there is a related widespread tendency to understand the divine and the human in competitive terms: they are thought to compete for the same space, in a way that means that the more human something is, the less divine it is, and vice versa. This is one basic aspect of the approach represented by Dawkins, in which God is purported to explain things in competition with science, which has led to God being seen as an unnecessary hypothesis that we are better off without. In biblical studies this sometimes appears as the notion that once one has provided as full as possible an account of the human origins and purposes of the biblical content and what its writers say about God, then nothing further either needs to be said or can be said about the possibility that the Bible's content might also originate from God.

So how can revelation be understood in a way that avoids these problems and is faithful to the Bible? One succinct and memorable formulation of the nature of revelation is provided by Nicholas Lash: "The search for God is not the search for comfort or tranquillity, but for truth, for justice, faithfulness, integrity: these, as the prophets tirelessly reiterated, are the forms of God's appearance in the world."[31] "The forms of God's appearance in the world"—that is, where God is revealed—are

31. Lash, "Creation, Courtesy, and Contemplation," in *The Beginning and the End of 'Religion,'* 179.

justice, faithfulness, and integrity. If so, then what does this envisage if the "natural" is to become also "supernatural"? The answer is surely when human lives are so receptive to, so graced by, God that they display God's own qualities. As a famous passage in Jeremiah says:

> Thus says the LORD: Do not let the wise boast in their wisdom, do not let the mighty boast in their might, do not let the wealthy boast in their wealth; but let those who boast boast in this, that they understand and know me, that I am the LORD; I act with steadfast love, justice, and righteousness in the earth, for in these things I delight, says the LORD. (Jer. 9:23–24 [Hebrew 9:22–23])

When human lives display steadfast love, justice, and righteousness, they display what matters more than the things that people customarily value (intelligence, strength, money), for they display God's own qualities.

Moreover, the Johannine portrayal of Jesus, which we have briefly considered, emphasizes a fundamental biblical understanding of revelation—namely, that whatever else God reveals, God supremely reveals *Himself*.[32] The divine is revealed in and through the human—supremely, Jesus. Again, it is in human life that is responsive to God, and so demonstrates the qualities and priorities of God, that God is to be encountered. The kind of knowledge that God gives is knowledge that enables human life to become what it is meant to be: not knowledge that "explains" the world in the manner of the natural sciences, but rather knowledge in the mode of *wisdom*, which, when rightly understood (and unlike what Jeremiah critiques), is a practical understanding of how to handle life well in accordance with

32. This is an issue where a Jew, looking to the Tanakh, might well express things differently, emphasizing the intrinsic importance of *torah* and *mitzvōt* ("law" and commandments). However, Jews and Christians are in agreement that the reception of God's revelation has fundamental implications for self-understanding and the living out of human life.

the realities of God's world. And this wisdom is embodied in a particular history, in the biblical record of God's call of a particular people to fulfill His good purposes in the world.

Our discussion of particular and privileged perspectives in chapter 3 entails that a belief in revelation involves attending to one particular context rather than to others—*Look here rather than there*—as the place where God is most clearly to be seen in the world. For Christians, Jesus supremely reveals God. But ancient Israel, as mediated through its authoritative writings, is also recognized by Christians as a particular context in which the God who is seen supremely in Jesus is already seen substantially and enduringly (and indeed, Jesus would not be rightly understood without this frame of reference).

For the concept of revelation to be meaningful, it is necessary to offer some account of what is involved in receiving revelation as revelation. If revelation involves responsiveness to God on the part of those who mediate it, then it requires further responsiveness on the part of others who would receive it, including an openness to "grace" (goodness, wonder, love) in whatever form it takes. More specifically, receiving revelation involves recognition and trust, a willingness to privilege certain people and writings and events and to enter into their reality for oneself.

The question of where one should place trust also entails the exercise of discernment; responsible trust requires, rather than dispenses with, the exercise of one's critical faculties. Moreover, the purpose of learning to see God in Jesus and in the context of Scripture is to enable one to see God elsewhere in the world and to live accordingly, with less self-deception than might otherwise be the case.

Revelation in Relation to Daniel 7 and Aeneid 1

How does such an understanding of revelation relate to the practices of biblical interpretation? A key point from the words of Jesus in John 7:16–17 is that teaching may be *not only* human *but also* from God. This in-principle understanding is applicable to other parts of the Bible also. It does not deny the fully human nature and content of the material, but sees these human dimensions as a vehicle for the self-communication of God.

It should always in principle be possible to give an explanation of the biblical text as indeed a human work, a human construction (a God dimension is not the part that appears humanly puzzling or inexplicable). Daniel 7 appears not to be the direct report of a visionary experience by its recipient, an exiled Jew named Daniel in Babylon, but rather represents the religious aspirations of unnamed Jews of the second century in Judea in their resistance to Antiochus Epiphanes. Although numerous details in any such account remain debatable—since, for example, much about the originating context of Daniel 7 is unknown for lack of surviving evidence—some such account can be seen as an in-principle comprehensive explanation in human terms. Yet this need not mean that the text and its content are *merely* human, such that they could not *also* be responsive to the antecedent initiative of God.

Should one, then, see the content of Daniel 7 as responsive to God and so in some sense not only human but also divinely given? That depends on the wider frame of reference one embraces and appropriates. One integral factor in the making of any such judgment about Daniel 7 is an evaluation of those qualities that the book of Daniel as a whole depicts in relation to the vision of God and the sovereignty He bestows: faithfulness in adversity (even to death), wisdom, and a trusting hope in the ultimate victory of the just God to whom the Jewish people look. This vision of God and of life is open to being taken up, in the context of the Christian Bible, into the vision of the sovereignty of the risen Christ and his commission to Christian disciples. Evaluation depends on perspective and location.

How might this apply to our comparison of *Aeneid* 1 with Daniel 7? It would be altogether too easy simply to claim that Jupiter, the Roman deity, is a false god, while the LORD, the God of Israel, is the true God—even if there is much readily understandable Christian precedent for doing that. Rather, the issue may be put differently. Are there elements of Virgil's vision that a believer in the God of Israel could affirm? The Virgilian vision of empire is moral, depicting the bringing of justice and peace and the overthrow of human arrogance (and it is dismaying that Augustine so swiftly dismisses this at the beginning of *City of God*, though clearly his polemical context affects what he says).[33] Insofar as this is so, then certain dimensions of the Virgilian vision can in principle be affirmed according to the same criteria whereby one would affirm the Daniel 7 (and wider biblical) vision as genuinely responsive to the initiative and leading of the one true God. This may also be a way of understanding Eliot's account of Virgil. Nonetheless, such affirmation is far from straightforward, as empire is such a complex and ambiguous phenomenon. There are particularly difficult complexities in discerning Virgil's vision of empire when one remembers not only the suffering of Jews and Christians at the hands of the pagan Roman Empire, but also the suffering of Jews and pagans at the hands of the christianized Roman Empire.

Conclusion

If the above account is on the right lines, then questions of divine revelation and belief in God need to be understood in ways other than an "all or nothing" or "here and nowhere else" mode. On the one hand, the biblical understanding of God is not meaningful if it is divorced from the life of a people called by God to live in such a way that they bear witness to Him in

33. See above, ch. 3, p. 117.

what they do and say. On the other hand, the God of Israel, believed in by Jews and Christians, is also the God of the whole world and can be discerned at work in the world beyond the boundaries of Jewish and Christian communities.

Among other things, this means that believers in God can both affirm and critique the life of the world around them. Put differently: many of those who come to faith in God will find that this brings with it an affirmation of the deepest moral intuitions and aspirations that they already had. That which they had deeply hoped and wanted to be true, the present sovereignty and the ultimate triumph of goodness and justice and wisdom, is now seen to have a particular embodiment which gives greater confidence that that ultimate truth really is true. To enter into faith not only confirms these intuitions but also enables them to be better lived and realized through growth in responsiveness to the God in whom these intuitions are realities. In Johannine terms, if Jesus is the Word "through whom all things were made" (John 1:3), then to come to faith is to come to a grasp of the way the world really is, to learn to be attuned to the rhythm of the universe.

Yet faith does not just confirm intuitions. It also challenges them. The fundamental intuitions of some people relate more to notions such as power and success than to goodness. Without an openness to being challenged, and a willingness to allow such intuitions to be modified and/or relinquished, faith for such people will be both distant and undesirable, something to be resisted. Moreover, even for those who do practice and hope for goodness, the Bible overturns expectations. The primacy of grace, for example—as seen in the God who calls the surprising and the unworthy—may not resonate naturally for many (at least with reference to others besides themselves). And as already noted, the central symbol of Christian faith, the cross—a symbol of execution whereby Jesus, in the prime of life, was put to death after being betrayed, abandoned, and tortured—challenges all natural assumptions about what God (if God really is there) ought to do, or to have done, to bring salvation to the world. If the very heart of the Christian Bible and of the Christian understanding of God is Jesus at Gethsemane, at Calvary, and outside the Easter tomb, then all easy notions of what it means to know God and to enter into the salvation of the world fall away.

In short, the purpose of privileging the Bible for faith in God is not to say, "Here is truth and elsewhere is error." Rather, it is a matter of being willing to learn, in light of the sovereignty of the crucified and risen Christ, ways of recognizing and responding appropriately to what is and is not of true value in God's world, wherever one may encounter it.

* 🟊 * ✦ * 🟊 * ✦ * 🟊 *

The Historical Framework for Richard Dawkins's Thinking and Its Conceptual Deficiencies

It is appropriate to give a little more space to some of the issues raised by Richard Dawkins. Dawkins writes with unfailing lucidity, and he articulates issues in ways that clearly make sense to many people in a disenchanted culture in which notions of faith and theology seem ever less comprehensible. As such, Dawkins represents a common contemporary mind-set. If my own positive thesis is to be grasped, it may help to show why at least some apparent objections are in fact misunderstandings.

Questions need to be put to Dawkins's definition of "God": "There exists a superhuman, supernatural intelligence who deliberately designed and created the universe and everything in it, including us."[1] The history of ideas that led to Dawkins's understanding of God is brilliantly set out by Michael Buckley in *At the Origins of Modern Atheism.* In brief, already in the seventeenth century the question of God steadily ceased to be a religious and existential issue, having ever less to do with trust in God in relation to Jesus and the Bible, and increasingly became instead a philosophical question. The question

1. Above, ch. 4, p. 131.

became whether there is evidence for the reality of God, and the keyword in relation to evidence was "design." Buckley sees Descartes and Newton "as the most influential figures at the dawn of modernity" and argues that they both "achieved a god commensurate with the evidence they explored. . . . In both of these philosophies, god functioned as an explanatory factor in a larger, more complete system. . . . Individual things needed explanation—ideas or individual facts—and god provided that explanation." Specifically with regard to Newton, Buckley summarizes: "The great argument, the only evidence for theism, is design, and experimental physics reveals that design."[2] This subsuming of theology into the natural sciences proved fatal for theology in due course.

One of the iconic moments in the history of modern atheism was an encounter in 1802 between Napoleon Bonaparte and Pierre Simon de Laplace, who advanced Newton's work in important ways (Laplace eventually became known as the "Newton of France"). Where Newton's approach had allowed for divine intervention to correct certain mechanical problems in the solar system, Laplace was able, by the principles of mechanics, to establish a dynamic stability that needed no divine intervention. Napoleon, speaking as a conventional Newtonian, referred to God as the author of certain celestial movements, to which Laplace is said to have replied, "I have no need of that hypothesis." His point was that the principles of mechanics must be mechanical, and that reference to the divine is simply irrelevant.[3] Thus the deity who provides explanations for natural phenomena on a par with those of the natural sciences becomes a "god of the gaps" who is steadily reduced to a vanishing point as the explanatory powers of the natural sciences develop.

2. Buckley, *At the Origins of Modern Atheism*, 348, 349, 202.
3. The story is contextualized in Buckley, *At the Origins of Modern Atheism*, 324–25.

That this is still Dawkins's own frame of reference is clear from two things.[4] On the one hand, there is his definition (above) of God as an "intelligence who deliberately designed and created the universe and everything in it"—that is, God represents a hypothesis about design in the universe. On the other hand, Dawkins is insistent (he repeats the point in various contexts) that he "could not imagine being an atheist at any time before 1859, when Darwin's *Origin of Species* was published."[5] Even if Laplace had eliminated God from physics, the situation was different for biology. William Paley's famous account of "evidences" for God from design was particularly influential in nineteenth-century Britain and provided Darwin's own initial frame of reference.[6] As a biologist, Dawkins makes the point that the apparent design of life within the world, which hitherto had been explained by appeal to God, could now, because of *Origin of Species*, be comprehensively accounted for in terms of natural selection. Thanks to Darwin, for Dawkins as for Laplace, God is a hypothesis that is no longer needed in light of scientific discovery. The fact that a line of Christian apologists up to Paley utilized this argument for God from design, and that this argument in one form or another still has not disappeared, has persuaded Dawkins to suppose that it is an intrinsic, authentic, and basic part of Christian belief.

But numerous theologians have shown how and why the argument from design is a corrupt mutation of Christian belief in creation, whose real meaning is quite different. As Nicholas Lash puts it, "The concept of creation . . . , for the scientist, seems

4. Dawkins is not alone in this. In ch. 1 I noted that H. L. Mencken was an articulate twentieth-century predecessor of Dawkins (above, p. 28). Mencken also maintained: "Religion, after all, is nothing but an hypothesis framed to account for what is evidentially unaccounted for." See Joshi, *H. L. Mencken on Religion*, 230.

5. Richard Dawkins, *The Blind Watchmaker: Why the Evidence of Evolution Reveals a Universe without Design* (New York: Norton, 1986), 4. Dawkins makes the point also in the 2006 "You Ask the Questions" feature in *The Independent*.

6. See above, ch. 3, pp. 86, 89.

primarily to refer to the establishment of the initial conditions of the world, whereas, for the Christian theologian, it simply acknowledges all things' absolute and intimate contingency."[7] Perhaps I may be permitted to cite my own recent discussion of "science and religion" in relation to Genesis 1, where I suggest that familiar discussions about the creation of the world might be illuminated by an analogy with the creation of a human person:

> A characteristic Christian (or Jewish or Muslim) affirmation that complements "God made the world" is "God has made me." What does, and does not, such an affirmation mean? Negatively, it does not mean that one's presence in the world is the result of something like a magician's trick, a sudden appearance without obvious explanation ("one moment I wasn't there, next moment I was"). That is, the claim to be made by God is not a denial of regular biological processes of conception from sperm and ovum, maturation within a womb, and birth after some nine months. Positively, the affirmation entails an understanding of both origin and destiny, in terms of coming from God and going to God. Its primary significance is in terms of what it means for a present existential understanding in the here and now. The affirmation seeks to express such existential realities as trust, accountability, dependence, contingency, the sense of oneself as a creature in relation to a creator.[8]

Such an account of creation is something Dawkins has consistently ignored, and so has not considered what difference it might make to his preferred account. One consequence, of course, is that the deity whose existence Dawkins is so keen to deny is not the God of the Bible or Christian faith in whom people can still believe and trust today.

7. See Lash, "On What Kinds of Things There Are," in *The Beginning and the End of 'Religion,'* 100.

8. R. W. L. Moberly, *The Theology of the Book of Genesis*, OTT (New York: Cambridge University Press, 2009), 64–65.

EPILOGUE:
TOWARDS BIBLICAL LITERACY

There is always more that could be said about the Bible and about expectations and approaches in relation to it. Nonetheless, I have, for better or worse, put forward my main thesis, and so it is almost time to stop.

I have offered a typology of three ways of approaching the Bible: as history, as classic, and as Scripture. This typology, while not comprehensive,[1] seeks to clarify both continuity and difference in varying contemporary approaches. Each of these three approaches seeks better understanding of the biblical text, and each is compatible with the others. A major difference between them is the goal for which understanding is sought—whether as an end in itself, valuable as any knowledge is valuable as an enhancement of life (history or classic), or as also a means to wisdom and the knowledge of God (Scripture); and a correlative of differing goals is the asking of different questions or the giving of different weight to shared questions. This distinction

1. For example, I have not discussed ideologically suspicious approaches, other than briefly and indirectly in excursus 1, despite their increase in recent years. Arguably, many of these form a distinct subset of approaches to the text as Scripture, since the premise for critiquing or seeking to disable use of the Bible is the understanding of believers that the Bible is still in some way authoritative for thought and life today.

between the approaches is not absolute, as great writings can affect their readers in unpredictable ways. Nonetheless, the distinction is real, since the Bible, approached as Scripture, is not only a text in a class or perhaps an exhibit on display but belongs also in the life of Christians as a fundamental resource for understanding the realities of God and of life.

This distinction can also be articulated in terms of the importance of context—the contexts not only of the biblical documents but also of their readers, and the bearing of the latter on decisions about criteria of interpretation and evaluation. One way of putting it might be: the narrower the contexts, the more straightforward the reading; the wider the contexts, the deeper and more variable the questions one poses and the more interesting the possible readings and evaluations that one may advance. The apparently simple comparison between *Aeneid* 1 and Daniel 7, as set out in chapter 1, and straightforward readings of each text, as given in chapter 2, need not just be ends in themselves, for they can also be seen to be implicated in assumptions and frames of reference that are complex and variegated, certain aspects of which are explored in chapters 3 and 4. The perspectives on life that people privilege, the role of plausibility structures, the potential of enduring literary works, the intrinsic challenge of the biblical notion of divine dominion with its human corollaries, and the possible grounds for believing that human words originate in God—all these enrich and enlarge one's reading and make apparent the difference between reading a text solely as history or classic, or also as Scripture. Benjamin Sommer, introducing his own recent work on the nature of Scripture and its authority in a Jewish context, nicely expresses an insight also central to my argument: "The most crucial differences between biblical critics and many theological interpreters of scripture occur not in the ways they read but in decisions they make before they begin reading at all."[2] The recognition and reception of documents as constitutive of Scripture, and not just as ancient history or cultural classics, makes a difference not only to how one reads but also to how the reading affects life.

The question of how the differing readings of the biblical material in these differing contexts should best be understood in relation to one another is a matter that is likely to keep interpreters, both scholarly and other, busy for the foreseeable future. It is integral to my thesis, however, that an argument for an approach to the Bible with constructive questions about God and faith on the agenda is not an imperialist claim that other approaches are invalid.

> In making a case for reading the biblical documents as Scripture, I have said relatively little about the action of God and the work of the Holy Spirit. This is essentially a strategic decision so as to focus on the necessary human corollaries and responses that make it possible for divine initiative to be received and understood and become fruitful.

One possible way of depicting my argument as a whole is that it is an attempt to draw on certain postmodern perspectives in such a way as to be able to reclaim and reformulate important premodern insights, and thereby offer an alternative to characteristic modern approaches without unlearning their hard-learned lessons and insights.

The Problem of Biblical Literacy

Before I finish, however, I would like to say a little about one particular recurring problem in discussions about the Bible: the problem of biblical literacy. By "literacy" I am not referring to good general knowledge of biblical content, which at present is declining in Europe and North America, even though some

2. Sommer, *Revelation and Authority*, 10.

biblical terms, images, and tropes continue to have a certain cultural resonance. Rather, I have in mind the ability to read the biblical text well, which is an issue, albeit in different forms, for all the respective approaches to the Bible as history, classic, and Scripture.[3]

There is a certain irony in the fact that, despite the prominence of the notion of reading the Bible "like any other book," people often read it in ways that do not characterize their general reading—not because they are seeking God and wisdom in and through its pages in a way that they might not with other books, but because they apparently do not know how to read it well, in terms of the working assumptions they should bring and the interpretive moves they should make.

For example, as already noted, it is hardly controversial to regard the Bible as at least a classic of Western culture. How, then, does one read a classic well? One regular assumption is that a work that has stood the test of time (which is, of course, a major part of the definition of what a classic is) deserves a certain respect, a certain benefit of the doubt (even though the question of which works count as classics, and why, is increasingly contested). If countless others have found a book worthwhile, then if we don't—at least on first reading—it may be that the problem lies in us more than in the book. The person who reads Virgil's *Aeneid* or Shakespeare's *King Lear* and pronounces them to be "rubbish" or "mistaken" or even just "boring" is likely to evoke reevaluation not of the *Aeneid* or *King Lear* but rather of their own quality of education and powers of judgment. Yet when it comes to the Bible, people often feel free to make quite sweeping negative judgments, as though doing so were indeed an evaluation of the Bible rather than of themselves.

3. There is a suggestive and penetrating analysis of the issue of biblical literacy, focused on the Old Testament but for the most part applicable also to the New Testament, in Brent Strawn's *The Old Testament Is Dying: A Diagnosis and Recommended Treatment* (Grand Rapids: Baker Academic, 2017).

Amos Oz on Jesus

Even sharp thinkers regularly perform below par when it comes to the Bible. Amos Oz, for example, is one of the finest of contemporary novelists, who in his fiction writes profoundly and searchingly about the modern state of Israel. In a recent interview for *The Tablet* (a Roman Catholic weekly journal) in relation to his most recent novel, *Judas*, he starts by speaking appreciatively about Jesus: "Jesus Christ is very close to my heart. I love his poetry. I love his wonderful sense of humour. I love his tenderness. I love his compassion. I have always regarded him as one of the greatest Jews who ever lived." However, he continues: "But Jesus Christ believes in universal love. He believes that the whole of humankind can live as one happy family. He believes we can quench our internal violence and prejudices and become better human beings. I don't." But where, I cannot but ask, does he find this in the New Testament? Certainly Jesus instructs his disciples, in various contexts, to love one another, their neighbors, and their enemies. But this is hardly "universal love" (unless carefully qualified), still less "the whole of humankind living as one happy family." Indeed, given the fact that in all the Gospels Jesus is portrayed as realizing that his ministry will lead to his being crucified, and does not encourage his disciples to suppose that they should fare better than their master does, Oz's is a rather strange construal to offer.

Oz further says, "I don't share Jesus' optimism. I don't share his famous idea of 'forgive them, they know not what they are doing.' I have no problem with forgiveness sometimes, but why would he say that, when we inflict pain on others, we don't know what we are doing?" The interviewer, Peter Stanford, observes that, by way of contrast with this, "Oz believes that, sometimes, we do [knowingly inflict pain on others], and this pessimistic take on human nature is at the very heart of his new novel."[4] Oz seems to be taking Jesus' words on the cross, in Luke's portrayal (Luke 23:34), as depicting an understanding that people generally should be forgiven for inflicting pain on others because they don't really know (or perhaps mean?) what they are doing. Well, one can read Jesus' words that way, even if only because Oz does. But it is at the very least an idiosyncratic reading, not only opting for one contestable construal of Jesus' words but also generalizing their sense beyond their immediate context (not to mention ignoring the text-critical problem of whether the words are really part of Luke's portrayal of Jesus, as they are absent in important ancient manuscripts).

The question of how best to take Jesus' words might reasonably give any careful reader a little pause. The referent of "them/they" is not specified: Is it Jewish authorities, Roman authorities, Roman soldiers, mocking onlookers, perhaps some combination, or perhaps all of them? A decision about the likely referent may make a difference to the likely sense of the whole. And on what basis does Oz think the words embrace people generally in other contexts ("when we inflict pain on others")? Likewise, the nature of the ignorance is not specified, and it can be read in several ways. It would be entirely plausible, for example, to see it as referring not to conscious awareness of inflicting pain, but rather to a failure to see the deeper purposes of God that are at work in Jesus. Oz's reading is, frankly, odd and implausible, even though he presents it as though it were the self-evident meaning of the text.

Oz takes the words in the way he does because he apparently sees Jesus as a lovable moral idealist who (unfortunately) does not really grasp the intractable nature of the human condition. Oz does not show the level of care and nuance in reading the Gospel narrative that I would have expected from so astute a

4. Peter Stanford, "The Tablet Interview: Uncompromising Voice for Uncomfortable Truth," interview with Amos Oz, *The Tablet*, October 8, 2016, 10–11.

writer, probably because his reading is unduly influenced by preconceptions drawn from discussions of Jesus and the Gospels in other contexts. Among other things, it suggests that reading the Bible well is not as straightforward an exercise as many would suppose.

Andrew Brown's Blog: Do Camels in Genesis Show That There Is Error in the Bible?

Another representative example comes from one of a myriad blogs relating to the Bible. The blog is that of Andrew Brown, an eminent journalist (and author) on the editorial board of *The Guardian*, one of the United Kingdom's main daily newspapers. He was previously the religion correspondent for *The Independent*, which for a number of years was also a main UK newspaper. He also does a (drily acerbic) report for *The Church Times* on each week's general religious press coverage. In other words, he is a well-educated and well-informed commentator on the contemporary religious scene. So if he writes a blog post on something to do with the Bible, one reasonably expects a high-quality, professional piece of writing.

The blog post I'm interested in, posted on February 13, 2014, is entitled "The Old Testament's Made-Up Camels Are a Problem for Zionism."[5] It has three main elements.

First, its basis is a recent discovery by two Israeli scholars who have worked on one particular site near modern Eilat in a search for camel bones, whose age can be established by radiocarbon dating. At this site these scholars found some domesticated camel bones, but none of these date from earlier than around 930↓. Brown adds a note that the skeleton of a domesticated camel can be distinguished from that of a wild camel on the basis of the thickness of the leg bones; if the leg

---

5. See https://www.theguardian.com/commentisfree/andrewbrown/2014/feb/13/old-testament-camels-zionism-genesis. I cite extracts from it here courtesy of Guardian News & Media Ltd.

bones are thickened, that is evidence that the camels were used for carrying heavy loads and so were domesticated.

Second, Brown uses this information to make some strong claims about the nature of the Old Testament and its content. His initial focus is on certain references to camels in the book of Genesis that, he says, we now know to be "made up" because there is a startling chronological mismatch: the camel bones found near Eilat, dating no earlier than ca. 930↓, are "about 1,500 years after the stories of the patriarchs in Genesis are supposed to have taken place." Brown cites two verses from Genesis 24, the story of Abraham's sending a servant to find a wife for Isaac, in which camels are mentioned. Although initially Brown says that the mention of camels here is "startlingly verisimilitudinous," he goes on to say that "whoever put the camels into [this] story . . . might as well have improved the story of Little Red Riding Hood by having her ride up to Granny's in an SUV." He then broadens his point to say that, although the work of these two Israeli scientists has "upset fundamentalists" (he alludes to some quotes in the *New York Times* that were presumably elicited in response to the publicizing of the find), "everyone else has known for decades that there is even less evidence for the historical truth of the Old Testament than there is for that of the Qur'an."

Finally, Brown directs his argument about the nature of the biblical material against contemporary Zionism, on the basis that the biblical material plays a foundational role in Zionism. "The idea of a promised land is based on narratives that assert with complete confidence stories that never actually happened." Although there can be other bases for Zionist concerns, Brown is clear that it is this biblical material that provides the emotional investment that in turn shapes Zionist politics.

So the moral of Brown's piece appears to be that Zionists, or at least those Zionists who are also fundamentalists, should become more honest about the Bible and its limitations, invest their emotions elsewhere, and change their politics accordingly.

What sparked Brown's writing this blog post? I imagine that it was a flurry of press features in the preceding days: perhaps a Fox News release entitled "Camel Bones Suggest Error in Bible, Archaeologists Say,"[6] or a piece in the *New York Times* entitled "Camels Had No Business in Genesis,"[7] though there was also a piece from *National Geographic* entitled "Domesticated Camels Came to Israel in 930 B.C., Centuries Later Than Bible Says,"[8] and other online material that might also have provided the spark.[9] All these articles refer to a 2013 essay, "The Introduction of Domestic Camels to the Southern Levant: Evidence from the Aravah Valley," by two Israeli scholars who work at Tel Aviv University, Lidar Sapir-Hen and Erez Ben-Yosef.[10] Fox News referred to "a press release announcing the research" which said that "in addition to challenging the Bible's historicity, this anachronism is direct proof that the text was compiled well after the events it describes." So there was apparently an attempt—successful, in the event—to generate publicity for research that otherwise might have remained in the decent obscurity of a learned journal, since the essay in question soberly keeps to its scholarly discussion of archaeological evidence. The wording "error in Bible" appears to be the publicity-generating phrase; after all, the claim that the text of Genesis was compiled "well after the events it describes," without further qualification, would be self-evidently the case even if one thought Moses to be the author of Genesis! Whether this wording was used by those issuing the press release, by

6. See http://www.foxnews.com/science/2014/02/06/camel-bones-suggest-error-in-bible.html.

7. See http://www.nytimes.com/2014/02/11/science/camels-had-no-business-in-genesis.html.

8. See http://news.nationalgeographic.com/news/2014/02/140210-domesticated-camels-israel-bible-archaeology-science/.

9. See http://phys.org/news/2014-02-archaeologists-date-domesticated-camels-israel.html.

10. *Tel Aviv* 40 (2013): 277–85.

those reporting on the event, or by both is unclear. In any case, this is the wording that apparently provokes fundamentalists and some Zionists and gives a certain tenor to the Fox News release, as also to Brown's blog post.

The Lack of Literacy in Brown's Discussion

Initial assumptions that Brown's blog post would be a quality piece of writing are rapidly overtaken by dismay at its display of a certain kind of biblical illiteracy.

One starting point might be to note that this "news" is hardly new. It is in fact a reasonably well-known and well-established scholarly contention that the occasional mention of camels in the narratives of the book of Genesis appears to be anachronistic. The essay by Sapir-Hen and Ben-Yosef is in no way trying to make a new claim about these references to camels as anachronistic, but rather is fine-tuning an existing scholarly understanding. Their starting point is: "Most scholars today agree that the dromedary was exploited as a pack animal sometime in the early Iron Age (not before the 12th century BCE)"; their argument is that new findings "enable us to pinpoint the introduction of domestic camels to the southern Levant more precisely."[11] The oldest item in their bibliography is W. F. Albright's 1949 book *The Archaeology of Palestine*. If we turn to this we read:

> In the eighteenth century B.C. the ass was the chief beast of burden. . . . There can be no doubt that wild camels were common in North Africa and south-western Asia in neolithic and chalcolithic times [roughly from the eighth millennium to late in the second millennium↓]. . . . Our oldest certain evidence for the domestication of the camel cannot antedate the end of the twelfth century B.C. These facts do not necessarily prove

11. Sapir-Hen and Ben-Yosef, "Introduction of Domestic Camels," 277, 282.

that earlier references to the camel in Genesis and Exodus are anachronistic, but they certainly suggest such an explanation.[12]

Comparably, Nahum Sarna, the author of a major commentary on Genesis,[13] introduces an extensive discussion of the camels in Genesis 24 thus: "The presence of the camel in this and other lists raises a complex problem"; and he follows Albright and others in saying that "all available evidence points to the conclusion that the effective domestication of the camel as a widely used beast of burden did not take place before the twelfth century B.C.E., which is a long time after the patriarchal period."[14] Since both Albright's study and Sarna's commentary are written for nonspecialist readerships ("the general public" in the editorial foreword to Albright's book, "the intelligent, educated layman" in Sarna's own introduction),[15] the sensationalizing presentation of the issue of anachronistic camels, as though this were a new discovery, is hardly warranted.

Second, there is also casual incoherence in Brown's presentation of the issue. His line about improving the story of Little Red Riding Hood "by having her ride up to Granny's in an SUV" is droll, and the introduction of a modern, technologically sophisticated vehicle into the premodern, rural context of Little Red Riding Hood would undoubtedly jar the sensibilities of any reader/hearer of the story. But on Brown's own account, the presence of camels in the story of Abraham's servant is "startlingly verisimilitudinous." If it is verisimilitudinous, then it fits and does not jar. This latter observation is clearly the right one, as most readers past and present have been unaware of

12. W. F. Albright, *The Archaeology of Palestine* (1949; repr., Harmondsworth, UK: Pelican, 1960), 206–7.

13. Nahum Sarna, *The JPS Torah Commentary: Genesis* (Philadelphia and Jerusalem: Jewish Publication Society, 1989).

14. Sarna, *Genesis*, 96.

15. Albright, *Archaeology of Palestine*, 6 (the editorial foreword is by Prof. M. Mallowan); Sarna, *Genesis*, xviii.

any problem in Genesis 24, not having the findings of modern archaeology to alert them. Brown's SUV analogy is inept and appears to be no more than an attempt to get a cheap laugh at how silly this bit of the Bible is.

Third, some of Brown's other terminology is also revealing. The term "made-up" appears both in the title and (twice) in the main text of the blog post, and he also speaks of the biblical material as "invented." Such terminology seems to be deliberately pejorative, along the lines of: "This stuff that some people believe in shouldn't be taken seriously, since it just came out of the heads of some exiled Jews." Then there is Brown's breathtaking dismissiveness about the Old Testament and "historical truth" *tout court*: "Everyone else [other than the fundamentalist] has known for decades that there is even less evidence for the historical truth of the Old Testament than there is for that of the Qur'an." Such rhetoric is of course difficult to analyze, not least because of its sweeping nature. And how many general readers are well informed about the kind of history there is within the Qur'an, and how best it is to be understood? But if Brown means that the Old Testament does not provide serious evidence for many centuries of the life of ancient Israel in its wider world, then he is just wrong. Most claims about the history of ancient Israel are currently contested. But to suggest that there is no evidence or history to be had is simply absurd.[16]

Fourth, there is a non sequitur in the material that Brown presents. The research by Sapir-Hen and Ben-Yosef to which he refers took place near Eilat, in the south of Israel. The story of Abraham's servant in Genesis 24 (which contains the vast majority of the camel references in Genesis) takes place in Aram

16. A fine survey both of the issues and of the literature relating to discussions of the history of Israel since the nineteenth century is Jean Louis Ska's "Questions of the 'History of Israel' in Recent Research," in *Hebrew Bible / Old Testament: The History of Its Interpretation*, vol. III/2, *The Twentieth Century—From Modernism to Post-Modernism*, ed. Magne Sæbø (Göttingen: Vandenhoeck & Ruprecht, 2015), 391–432.

Naharaim (which is specified in that part of the biblical text actually cited by Brown)—a region in Mesopotamia some 500 miles to the north of Eilat. Unless it is made clear, as Brown does not, that there is widespread evidence to suggest that the camel was not domesticated before the twelfth century↓, a reader may be forgiven for asking, "Why should what was the case around Eilat, in a desert region, determine what may or may not have been the case some 500 miles away, in a fertile region closer to historic Mesopotamian civilizations?"

> Unfortunately, the discussion above does not exhaust the problems in Brown's presentation. For example, he does not clearly distinguish, and then appropriately interrelate, the archaeological issue of the date of the camel bones, the "world within the text" issue of the likely date envisaged for Genesis 24's story, and the "world behind the text" issue of the likely date of the story's formation and composition. Rather, Brown muddles the issues, apparently for the sake of rhetorical effect. But it should already be clear that his blog post is both confused and misleading and, as such, is sadly illustrative of the wider problem that people who should know better too easily perform badly when discussing the Bible and produce a discourse with more heat than light.

Towards Understanding the Camels in Genesis

In light of all this, how best might the mention of camels in Genesis be understood? As with so many issues in ancient history, there is no one or obvious way of tackling the question, but there are a number of possible approaches, of which I mention three.

The first is to ask whether it might yet be the case that references to camels in Genesis are not anachronistic. This is the approach of Nahum Sarna, whose clear recognition of the historical difficulties has already been cited. He suggests this resolution:

> The original habitat of the camel seems to have been Arabia. It is likely that the domesticated camel at first spread very slowly

and long remained a rarity. A wealthy man might acquire a few as a prestige symbol for ornamental rather than utilitarian purposes. This would explain their presence in Abraham's entourage, their nonuse as beasts of burden, and their special mention in situations where wealth and honor need to be displayed, as, for instance, in Genesis 24 [a marriage negotiation].[17]

Such a scenario would appear to be fully compatible with the findings of Sapir-Hen and Ben-Yosef; although conjectural, it is a plausible conjecture.

A second approach is to appeal to the commonplace nature of a certain amount of anachronism in much (especially traditional) storytelling, in which the past receives some of the colors of the present. This is in essence the approach of Albright in the way he continues his account of the problem that has already been cited: "Of course, such anachronisms in local colour no more disprove the historicity of the underlying tradition than Tissot's painted scenes of Bible life falsify the biblical story by depicting its heroes as modern Palestinian Arabs."[18] To observe that elements of a story are technically anachronistic would presumably meet with little more than a shrug ("So?") from many a storyteller. The presence of such a convention within biblical storytelling need not be startling.

A third possible approach is to see the content of Genesis 24 as deriving from the time and place of its author. This appears to be essentially Brown's position, though the option is potentially more subtle and interesting than he implies. An author's concerns can be imaginatively set in an ancient time, and the interest and possible truth content of the story lie in the handling of those concerns. For example, this appears to be the case with the narrative that opens the book of Job (Job 1–2). Here the setting of the story seems to be a kind of ancient "patriarchal"

17. Sarna, *Genesis*, 96.
18. Albright, *Archaeology of Palestine*, 207.

setting in which, interestingly, Job possesses (among many other things) numerous camels (Job 1:3). However, the issues probed within the story are those of its storyteller—especially the question of how to test whether exemplary fear of God (in Christian terms, faith in God) is really what it appears to be. It is a moot point whether the patriarchal narratives generally are of the same genre as the Job narrative, even if some of them might be. Genesis 24, with all its camels, is primarily a story about God's guidance of Abraham's faithful servant, who is both astute and open to God.

My concern is not so much to resolve the issue of the camels as it is to give some sense of some of the ways it can be responsibly tackled without resorting to sensational claims about "error in the Bible," which do not contribute to a better grasp of what is at stake in reading these ancient and enduring texts well.

Error and Trust in Relation to the Bible

Why do some educated and intelligent people perform below par when it comes to discussing the Bible and its content? Although there are no doubt many contributory factors, one seemingly clear element of provocation, both in Brown's blog and in some of the other press releases related to Sapir-Hen and Ben-Yosef's research, is the cultural presence of "fundamentalists" and of those who deny that there is "error" in the Bible. "Fundamentalist" is typically such an imprecise and usually abusive term, used in such a wide range of ways and contexts, that I will leave it aside here. But it is important to note the cultural presence of those believers for whom the notion of "error" in the Bible is problematic, such that the Bible should be understood to be without error. This contention seems to function, in some contexts, rather like certain insects that irritatingly and distractingly buzz around one's face and food during an outdoor meal—that is, it exasperates and provokes those who disagree into wanting, whenever possible, to take a swipe and to point out that there *are* errors in the Bible. Hence the interesting but hardly exceptional archaeological research of Sapir-Hen and Ben-Yosef is promoted with press releases that grandly announce that there is "error in the Bible," a claim that then receives international press coverage despite the nonconcern with this issue in the essay itself, and the less-than-novel nature of the claim.

A belief in the inerrancy of the Bible, like a belief in the infallibility of the Pope, is, in its best and strongest form, a much more sophisticated and carefully focused understanding than might be gathered from many of its popular proponents or opponents. This is presumably why the respective beliefs about the Bible and the Pope have been articulated and persist, despite the ridicule they often attract. My present concern is to join neither the advocates nor the detractors. However, I should say that I am unpersuaded that what is most important about the Bible—in relation to God and to truth and wisdom about human life and destiny—is usefully and helpfully clarified or defended by the contention that the Bible contains no error. As already seen in relation to the use of the work of Sapir-Hen and Ben-Yosef, concerns about "error in the Bible" can too easily skew an understanding of what is really at stake in biblical interpretation. Moreover, concerns about error are particularly at home in the context of an evidentialist approach to the Bible, to which I am trying to articulate an alternative.

Put briefly: "trustworthy" is a richer, deeper, and more appropriate term for (would-be) believers to apply to the Bible than "inerrant." It expresses the self-identifying stance of the Christian churches that both their thought and their practice are appropriately rooted in the content of the Bible. Trustworthiness has to do with the existential openness that is necessary for finding God, or being found by God, in and through the pages of the Bible. The notion of trustworthiness is also robust, as it is not a matter of all or nothing or of slippery slopes. An affirmation of trustworthiness, whatever qualifications or caveats may accompany it, is the basis for the confident expectations with which (would-be) believers may seek truth, albeit often uncomfortable truth, about God, the world, and themselves in the Bible. We know in life generally that the placing of trust requires the recipient to have qualities that make for reliability, and that their possible intellectual limitations and deficiencies may be irrelevant to their reliability. Importantly, the real problem for trust is not error but deception. It is deception, rather than error, that entails substantive moral and spiritual failure such as makes trust inappropriate.[19] Moreover, as already noted, established trust is not incompatible with the asking of searching questions, but rather can set the context for it.

So I would like to conclude this proposal for reading the Bible today as "the lively oracles of God" and "the most valuable thing that this world affords" with some preliminary guidelines for reading the Bible well, in keeping with a recognition of it as trustworthy.

Some Hermeneutical Guidelines for Reading Scripture Well

Some Hermeneutical Implications of the Biblical Canon

Some of the hermeneutical implications of the biblical canon have already been mentioned and so need no more than summary reminder here. The canon—which I am using here as convenient shorthand for a range of factors involved in approaching ancient documents as Scripture—is integral to interpreting the Bible *unlike* any other book. The canon has to

---

19. Some of the wider issues here are helpfully discussed by Onora O'Neill in her 2002 BBC Reith Lectures, *A Question of Trust* (Cambridge: Cambridge University Press, 2002), esp. 61–100.

do with the Christian church's *privileging* the Bible and its contents, and with the church's role as a *plausibility structure* for approaching the Bible with *expectations* about the value of what one can find there, especially in relation to God, that one does not have of other documents (however valuable in their own way they may be). Canon also necessarily involves the *recontextualization* of once-independent documents into a particular collection that creates its own context of meaning, such that documents will to some extent acquire meanings and resonances that may not have been envisaged or available when they were first written.

Some further implications, not yet explicitly noted, may also briefly be spelled out. When the canon is located in the context of Christian life, one inevitable consequence is the generation of a "rule of faith." In a sense this is a natural consequence of recontextualization, when the context of individual documents shifts from their historical context of origin to a new literary/canonical context of preservation and privileging. This new context generates questions about how best to relate the documents to one another, and it becomes important to offer some kind of synthetic understanding of the whole. The community that is committed to this material learns to articulate a general sense of what it is about and why it matters—a sense of "how things go" in a Christian frame of reference. Thus it is natural to codify this general understanding in one way or another so that those who come newly to faith, as children or converts, are not left to their own devices to work out for themselves what it is all about—that is, people are not encouraged to come to the Bible with a tabula rasa, but are given a clear working frame of reference from the outset. The historic creeds are probably the best-known examples of such a rule of faith, in that they offer a kind of guide to what is in the Bible and are focused on God as known in and through Jesus (though the creeds were framed in response to particular controversies and omit much, especially in relation to the Old Testament). All the major churches also have further traditions of thought and practice—liturgies, confessional summaries, authoritative expositions, artistic depictions, hymns, musical compositions, and suchlike—that induct believers into particular ways of understanding the Bible and its implications for life.

It is sometimes held that to read the Bible in an ecclesial context with a rule of faith is to make biblical study dull and predictable, subject to a priori dogmatic decrees and terminally oriented towards homiletic exhortations. Of course that may happen. But it need not. If God really is the ground of all reality, understanding God via the Bible will necessarily be demanding. In the Bible and in Christian faith, both God and humanity intrinsically constitute a mystery, not in the sense of a puzzle awaiting resolution (as in a detective mystery)—though any gain in knowledge can be helpful—but in the sense of a reality the depth of whose dimensions is best appreciated only as one engages with it: "The more you know, the more you know you don't know." To grow into this reality, and to study it appropriately, is the work of a lifetime (and perhaps beyond).

Nonetheless, a basic corollary of such rules of faith needs highlighting. Rules of faith direct (would-be) believers to what is of central importance in terms of faith, hope, and love, but pass over many issues in silence. However, contemporary hot-button debates about gender and sexuality are proving contentious and difficult to resolve partly because their relationship to central priorities of faith is unclear and can be argued in more than one way. They also revolve around changing existential self-understandings of contemporary men and women. For example, certain assumptions about gender and gender roles were so firmly in place for the biblical writers that many contemporary challenges that arise from the emancipation of women in the Western world over the last couple of centuries not only were not envisaged but also were implicitly excluded as legitimate issues by the acceptance of those assumptions. The question of what counts as a faithful understanding and use of the biblical documents as Scripture for today is less than straightforward, insofar as it is necessary to question and depart from some of those ancient assumptions.[20] As argued in the previous chapter, continuity with ancient understandings and practices of faith is not the same as identity with them.

Literary Competence and Imaginative Seriousness

It may be appropriate at this point to say a little more about the issue raised in the introduction—that is, how best to understand the genres of the biblical text and their relation to varying conceptions of history. One legacy of historical-critical work on the Bible is a sharper recognition of the possible difference and distance between what I have been referring to throughout this book as "the world within the text" and "the world behind the text." Premodern biblical scholarship tended to assume that there was little difficulty here, and focused elsewhere. But the growth of a sharper historical awareness and questioning in the seventeenth and eighteenth centuries led to the first real recognition of a problem—a gap, so it appeared, between narrative and reality, as famously depicted by Hans Frei in *The Eclipse of Biblical Narrative*.[21] The characteristic modern handling of the problem has been to privilege "the world behind the text" (reality) over "the world within the text" (narrative), and to see the value of the latter in terms of the extent to which it contributes to a clearer sense of the former, rather than to see the narrative itself as the meaningful and enduringly significant depiction of reality.

20. A suggestive account of principled negotiation of difficulties in the Bible is Ellen F. Davis's "Critical Traditioning: Seeking an Inner Biblical Hermeneutic," in *The Art of Reading Scripture*, ed. Ellen F. Davis and Richard B. Hays (Grand Rapids: Eerdmans, 2003), 163–80.

21. New Haven and London: Yale University Press, 1974.

One result of this modern approach has been the privileging of the term "history" to depict the factually reliable reality that may ideally underlie the biblical narrative. Much scholarly writing about the Bible seems to operate with the assumption that reality in the past should be designated "history," and that the biblical text as it stands is a kind of history manqué—or, in the more strongly negative formulation of Spinoza, whose approach to the Bible in his 1670 *Theologico-Political Treatise* stands, as already noted, at the root of modern historical-critical work: "The history of the Bible is not so much imperfect as untrustworthy."[22] Consequently, scholars have often tried to find some literary categorization other than "history" for the biblical narrative itself, even while recognizing that some parts of it might still qualify as "historical." Hence a constant quest for other categories for the biblical text—both more general categorizations, such as "tradition" or "story" or "narrative" or "theology," and more specific categorizations, such as "saga" or "folktale" or "legend" or "myth." In either case, the value of the biblical text in itself has tended to be deprivileged in relation to the history that should ideally be extractable from it.

Many Christians, unhappy that the value of the biblical text is apparently being impugned, have unfortunately not challenged the conceptual frame of reference within which the problem was set up—that is, they accepted that what really mattered was to attain the historically reliable—but instead have argued that the biblical narrative already indeed had/has the necessary historical reliability. They have tried to close the gap between text and referent and to argue that there is no real (or only minimal) difference between the world within the text and the world behind the text.

One advantage of referring to "the world within the text" and "the world behind the text" (and also "the world in front

22. Spinoza, *A Theologico-Political Treatise*, in Elwes, *Benedict de Spinoza*, 120.

of the text"), and a primary reason for my adopting the terminology throughout this book, is that such terminology (as also the more narrowly focused technical terms "synchronic" and "diachronic") does not implicitly privilege one world over the other, but is a helpful reminder that there are necessarily different dimensions involved in understanding, and perhaps appropriating, the Bible (as also the *Aeneid*). Good reading needs these distinctions. Of course, the world within the text has an obvious priority for most readers, especially readers of the Bible, as it is what they actually encounter on the page, whether in church or at home. But learning to read well involves recognizing that there is usually more to good reading than one initially supposed.

These issues can also be approached from a different angle. In contemporary culture, narrative (whether on the page or on the big or little screen) and reality relate to each other in many and varied ways, and people are usually untroubled by this. Both fiction and nonfiction work in many ways that often overlap, and the criteria by which we judge their value vary according to the nature of the material. If we are at home in the culture, we are generally at ease with its literary and cinematic conventions, even though, of course, sometimes we may be uncertain about the genre of what we are reading or seeing, and authors and producers can sometimes play with and challenge our working assumptions. Yet when people read the Bible, a certain rigidity easily sets in, and the question "Did it happen?," which can be treated as equivalent to "Is it true?," readily comes to the fore and relegates questions about the conventions of the genre and the nature of the subject matter of the text to a secondary position, if they feature at all. In short, in contemporary culture, people are generally at ease with a diversity of genres in storytelling and are happy to recognize differing kinds of value in the differing genres. And the novel has become a powerful vehicle, at least in the hands of its best practitioners, for exploring and articulating truth about life. But with the Bible, people can feel less at home in relation to its literary conventions (how many are widely read in premodern literature?), and, at least among believers, its sacred status can sometimes make for a certain lack of confidence in handling it (i.e., readers don't want to "get it wrong"); so if a narrative appears realistic and history-like, then maybe the appropriate default assumption is that it is history.

If literature can portray reality in many ways through a variety of genres, then it should not be a problem to recognize such variety in the Bible. Familiarity with premodern literature shows the range and persistence of genres that we label as folktale, legend, myth, or suchlike (though these labels can be clumsy and lacking nuance, and they do not do justice to the movie-like presentation by the narrator that runs through the different biblical narrative genres). The persistence of such genres likely indicates that they were found to be meaningful and accessible to those who produced and received them; and some of the material thus labeled has probably been more enduring in impact than anything we label "history." In theological terms, there should be no in-principle objection to the notion that God could make use of—that is, inspire—such meaningful genres of literature for the instruction of His people.[23]

Perhaps the most widely read theological writer of the twentieth century was C. S. Lewis (though, disappointingly, because he was a professional scholar of literature who wrote popular theology, rather than a professional theologian, he usually is not included in surveys of twentieth-century theology).[24] Because of his deep immersion in literature down the ages, he was able to be relaxed and positive about the recognition of various genres in

23. A significant recent account of biblical inspiration that shares much common ground with my own account is Stephen B. Chapman's "Reclaiming Inspiration for the Bible," in *Canon and Biblical Interpretation*, ed. Craig Bartholomew et al., Scripture and Hermeneutics Series 7 (Milton Keynes, UK: Paternoster, 2006), 167–206.

24. For example, he is unmentioned in *The Christian Theologians: An Introduction to Christian Theology since 1918*, ed. David Ford and Rachel Muers, 3rd ed. (Oxford: Blackwell, 2005).

Scripture and their theological implications: "I think He meant us to have sacred myth and sacred fiction as well as sacred history."[25]

Recognition of the diversity of literary genres in Scripture should be liberating for readers, who are thus free to follow the material on its own terms and to read it with full imaginative seriousness in terms of its story line and subject matter, without feeling obliged to be like Procrustes and make it fit, willy-nilly, into the modern categories of "history" and "factual authenticity."[26] Put differently: entering into the world within the text with full imaginative seriousness should not, in principle, be diminished by critical judgments about the genre of the text and the putative world behind the text. The difference that should be made by such critical awareness relates to recognizing which questions a text will and will not constructively sustain, and to determining the uses to which a text is and is not best put.

Conclusion

One of my fundamental concerns has been to show something of what is involved in having faith/belief/trust in relation to what the Bible says about God, Jesus, and life in this world. I have argued that a key issue has to do with where one places one's trust in life and why, given that all have to place trust somewhere. Although questions of trust should of course be appropriately rational,

25. The context of Lewis's words is reflection on the types of literature in the Old Testament in relation to why he was not a "fundamentalist" (C. S. Lewis, *Collected Letters*, vol. 3, *Narnia, Cambridge, and Joy, 1950–1963*, ed. Walter Hooper [London: HarperCollins, 2006], 652–53). Lewis's understanding of Scripture, together with his strong appreciation of the genre of myth and his disappointment that so many people read the Bible with a poor literary sensibility, is usefully set out in Kevin Vanhoozer, "On Scripture," in *The Cambridge Companion to C. S. Lewis*, ed. Robert MacSwain and Michael Ward (Cambridge: Cambridge University Press, 2010), 75–88.

26. Procrustes is a figure from Greek mythology, a robber who attacked and abducted people and made them fit into his iron bed either by stretching them or by cutting off body parts. He has become a byword for those who insist on making other people or things fit their own preconceptions.

and open to empirical and scientific evidence where relevant, they nonetheless transcend the purely rational and engage the whole person in ways that can often be difficult to analyze. Crucial to the placing of trust is the influence of "significant others" and the related matter of which features of life and the world one privileges and allows to become the key to one's own understanding and practice of life. This entails also some recognition of which difficulties one is prepared to live with. Christian belief is a matter of recognizing Jesus in the New Testament as the person who supremely makes sense of (without "explaining") life in the world and God, of being willing to trust the biblical portrayal of Jesus as a figure who not only belongs to the past but who is also a living reality now, and of being part of those communities who seek to realize in everyday life what that reality of Jesus might mean, thereby offering grace and hope—and where necessary, warning—to others. The Bible is a lens for making sense of the world in terms of overall understanding ("God's world"), identity ("our/my story"), and purpose and destiny ("we are made by and for God"), with all the consequences for living well that follow. This is without prejudice to the other understandings of the world that are available through history and the sciences, even though the negotiation of differing understandings and identities can often be demanding.

I hope that my argument has also indicated that there is more than one way of framing issues of the truth of biblical content in relation to the work of critical biblical scholarship and modern knowledge generally. I have focused predominantly on just two biblical passages, Daniel 7 and Matthew 28, each of which portrays a similar scenario: an assurance of an ultimate triumph that is both divine and human, in which qualities such as justice and goodness are vindicated. In each case the triumph is mediated via an interim divine bequest to particular human recipients, a bequest that either implies or states explicitly what these recipients should be doing until that ultimate triumph is realized. Daniel 7 portrays a vision in a dream; Matthew 28 is a narrative of an encounter in Galilee. In each case, however, the nature of the literary genre is open to question. Does Daniel 7 recount an actual vision in a dream, or is the vision a graphic expression of a particular assurance for persecuted Jews? Does Matthew 28 recount actual words of the risen Jesus, or is the encounter between the risen Jesus and his disciples on the mountaintop in Galilee a concretized depiction of early Christian convictions? In each case, differing judgments about the nature of the text can be defended. But even if the contention be entirely granted that both episodes use a creative literary vehicle in order to depict a particular understanding of God's ultimate sovereignty, that should not prevent each scenario from being engaged with full imaginative and existential seriousness. Further, such a contention does not resolve the most important question posed by the content of each passage: *Is it true?* Is the deity depicted a construct of the human imagination, or is the deity in fact the living God? Does God ultimately vindicate His persecuted faithful? Is all authority in heaven and on earth given to the risen Jesus? Is it important for people to live now in ways that embody those qualities that will ultimately be vindicated? And is it right to see the realization of Daniel's vision of the Ancient One as enfolded within, and transformed by, Matthew's portrayal of the unlimited authority and significance of the risen Jesus?

To give a nonsimplistic answer to such questions is by no means easy. I have tried to indicate some of the ingredients that should go into a responsible Christian answer, though of course there is more that could be said. Ultimately, however, in line with John 7:16–17, the truth and trustworthiness of the biblical witness, and of its possible origin in God, cannot be known without a readiness, alongside other believers past and present, to respond, to enter with faith into the content of that witness, and to live and die accordingly.

BIBLIOGRAPHY

Albright, W. F. *The Archaeology of Palestine*. Reprint, Harmondsworth, UK: Pelican, 1960.

Alter, Robert. *The Art of Biblical Narrative*. London: Allen & Unwin, 1981.

———. *Canon and Creativity: Modern Writing and the Authority of Scripture*. New Haven: Yale University Press, 2000.

———. *The Five Books of Moses: A Translation with Commentary*. New York and London: Norton, 2004.

Augustine. *The City of God*. Translated by William Babcock. Edited by Boniface Ramsey. The Works of Saint Augustine I/6. New York: New City Press, 2012.

———. *The Manichean Debate*. Translated by Roland Teske. Edited by Boniface Ramsey. The Works of Saint Augustine I/19. Hyde Park, NY: New City Press, 2006.

———. *Sermons*. Translated by Edmund Hill, OP. Edited by John E. Rotelle, OSA. The Works of Saint Augustine III/4. Brooklyn: New City Press, 1992.

Bagnall, Roger S., and Bruce W. Frier. *The Demography of Roman Egypt*. Cambridge: Cambridge University Press, 1994.

Barr, James. "Jowett and the Reading of the Bible 'Like Any Other Book.'" In *Bible and Interpretation: The Collected Essays of James Barr*. Vol. 1, *Interpretation and Theology*, edited by John Barton, 169–97. Oxford: Oxford University Press, 2013.

Beard, Mary. *Confronting the Classics: Traditions, Adventures and Innovations*. London: Profile, 2013.

———. *SPQR: A History of Ancient Rome.* London: Profile, 2015.

Berger, Peter L. *The Social Reality of Religion.* London: Faber & Faber, 1969.

Berger, Peter L., and Thomas Luckmann. *The Social Construction of Reality: A Treatise in the Sociology of Knowledge.* New York: Doubleday, 1967.

Braund, Susanna Morton. "Virgil and the Cosmos: Religious and Philosophical Ideas." In *The Cambridge Companion to Virgil*, edited by Charles Martindale, 204–21. Cambridge: Cambridge University Press, 1997.

Brock, Sebastian. "The Guidance of St. Ephrem: A Vision to Live By." In *The Practice of the Presence of God: Theology as a Way of Life*, edited by Martin Laird and Sheelah Treflé Hidden, 109–19. London and New York: Routledge, 2017.

Brown, Andrew. "The Old Testament's Made-Up Camels Are a Problem for Zionism." *The Guardian* (blog), February 13, 2014. https://www.the guardian.com/commentisfree/andrewbrown/2014/feb/13/old-testament -camels-zionism-genesis.

Bryan, Christopher. *Render to Caesar: Jesus, the Early Church, and the Roman Superpower.* New York: Oxford University Press, 2005.

Buckley, Michael. *At the Origins of Modern Atheism.* New Haven and London: Yale University Press, 1987.

Camps, W. A. *An Introduction to Virgil's Aeneid.* Oxford: Oxford University Press, 1969.

Carroll, Robert P. *Wolf in the Sheepfold: The Bible as a Problem for Christianity.* London: SPCK, 1991.

Chapman, Stephen B. "Collections, Canons, and Communities." In *The Cambridge Companion to the Hebrew Bible / Old Testament*, edited by Stephen B. Chapman and Marvin A. Sweeney, 28–54. New York: Cambridge University Press, 2016.

———. "Reclaiming Inspiration for the Bible." In *Canon and Biblical Interpretation*, edited by Craig Bartholomew et al., 167–206. Scripture and Hermeneutics Series 7. Milton Keynes, UK: Paternoster, 2006.

Childs, Brevard S. *Old Testament Theology in a Canonical Context.* London: SCM, 1985.

Clines, David J. A. "Metacommentating Amos." In *Interested Parties: The Ideology of Writers and Readers of the Hebrew Bible*, 76–93. JSOTSup 205. Sheffield, UK: Sheffield Academic, 1995.

Collins, John J. *Daniel.* Hermeneia. Minneapolis: Fortress, 1993.

Cook, Stephen L. "Apocalyptic Writings." In *The Cambridge Companion to the Hebrew Bible / Old Testament*, edited by Stephen B. Chapman and Marvin A. Sweeney, 331–48. New York: Cambridge University Press, 2016.

Cottingham, John. *How to Believe*. London and New York: Bloomsbury, 2015.

———. *Why Believe?* London and New York: Continuum, 2009.

Cunningham, M. P., ed. *Aurelii Prudentii Clementis Carmina*. CCSL 126. Turnholt: Brepols, 1966.

Darwin, Charles. "Autobiography." In *The Life and Letters of Charles Darwin, Including an Autobiographical Chapter*, edited by Francis Darwin, 1:26–107. London: John Murray, 1887.

Darwin, Francis, ed. *The Life and Letters of Charles Darwin, Including an Autobiographical Chapter*. 2 vols. London: John Murray, 1887.

Davies, Philip R. *Whose Bible Is It Anyway?* JSOTSup 204. Sheffield, UK: Sheffield Academic, 1995.

Davis, Ellen F. "Critical Traditioning: Seeking an Inner Biblical Hermeneutic." In *The Art of Reading Scripture*, edited by Ellen F. Davis and Richard B. Hays, 163–80. Grand Rapids: Eerdmans, 2003.

Dawkins, Richard. *The Blind Watchmaker: Why the Evidence of Evolution Reveals a Universe without Design*. New York: Norton, 1986.

———. *The God Delusion*. London: Bantam, 2006.

———. *River Out of Eden: A Darwinian View of Life*. London: Weidenfeld & Nicholson, 1995.

———. "You Ask the Questions." *The Independent*, December 4, 2006. http://www.independent.co.uk/news/people/profiles/richard-dawkins -you-ask-the-questions-special-427003.html.

Desmond, Adrian, and James Moore. *Darwin*. London: Michael Joseph, 1991.

Driver, S. R. *Daniel*. CBSC. Cambridge: Cambridge University Press, 1905.

———. *Introduction to the Literature of the Old Testament*. ITC. Edinburgh: T&T Clark, 1897.

Edwards, Katie, ed. *Rethinking Biblical Literacy*. New York: Bloomsbury T&T Clark, 2015.

Ehrman, Bart, ed. *The New Testament and Other Early Christian Writings: A Reader*. New York: Oxford University Press, 1998.

Eliot, T. S. "Virgil and the Christian World." In *On Poetry and Poets*, 121–31. London: Faber & Faber, 1957.

————. "What Is a Classic?" In *On Poetry and Poets*, 53–71. London: Faber & Faber, 1957.

Elwes, R. H. M., ed. and trans. *Benedict de Spinoza: "A Theologico-Political Treatise" and "A Political Treatise."* New York: Dover, 1951.

Epstein, I., ed. *The Babylonian Talmud: Seder Mo'ed*. Vol. 1, *Shabbath*. London: Soncino, 1938.

Fagles, Robert. *The Aeneid*. New York: Penguin, 2008.

Farrar, F. W. *History of Interpretation*. 1885 Bampton Lectures. London: Macmillan, 1886.

Ford, David, and Rachel Muers, eds. *The Christian Theologians: An Introduction to Christian Theology since 1918*. 3rd ed. Oxford: Blackwell, 2005.

Fox, Robin Lane. *Pagans and Christians*. Harmondsworth, UK: Viking, 1986.

Fox News. "Camel Bones Suggest Error in Bible, Archaeologists Say." February 6, 2014. http://www.foxnews.com/science/2014/02/06/camel-bones -suggest-error-in-bible.html.

Frei, Hans. *The Eclipse of Biblical Narrative*. New Haven and London: Yale University Press, 1974.

Goldingay, John. *Daniel*. WBC 30. Dallas: Word, 1989.

Grabbe, Lester L. "A Dan(iel) for All Seasons: For Whom Was Daniel Important?" In *The Book of Daniel: Composition and Reception*, edited by John J. Collins and Peter W. Flint, 1:229–46. Leiden: Brill, 2002.

Hagendahl, Harald. *Augustine and the Latin Classics*. 2 vols. Göteborg: Elanders Bohtryckeri Aktiebolag, 1967.

Harrison, Peter. *The Territories of Science and Religion*. Chicago and London: University of Chicago Press, 2015.

Hays, Christopher B. *Hidden Riches: A Sourcebook for the Comparative Study of the Hebrew Bible and Ancient Near East*. Louisville: Westminster John Knox, 2014.

Hays, Richard B. *Echoes of Scripture in the Gospels*. Waco: Baylor University Press, 2016.

Hinchliff, Peter. *Benjamin Jowett and the Christian Religion*. Oxford: Clarendon, 1987.

Hollinger, Dennis. "The Church as Apologetic: A Sociology of Knowledge Perspective." In *Christian Apologetics in the Postmodern World*, edited by Timothy R. Phillips and Dennis L. Okholm, 182–93. Downers Grove, IL: InterVarsity, 1995.

Jenkins, Philip. *The Next Christendom: The Coming of Global Christianity*. 3rd ed. Oxford: Oxford University Press, 2011.

Jenson, Robert. *Canon and Creed*. Interpretation: Resources for the Use of Scripture in the Church. Louisville: Westminster John Knox, 2010.

———. "Hermeneutics and the Life of the Church." In *Reclaiming the Bible for the Church*, edited by Carl Braaten and Robert Jenson, 89–105. Edinburgh: T&T Clark, 1995.

Joshi, S. T., ed. *H. L. Mencken on Religion*. Amherst, NY: Prometheus, 2002.

Jowett, Benjamin. "On the Interpretation of Scripture." In *Essays and Reviews: The 1860 Text and Its Reading*, edited by Victor Shea and William Whitla, 477–536. Charlottesville and London: University Press of Virginia, 2000.

Keate, Georgie. "How Aylan's Death Really Did Change World's View." *The Times*, January 11, 2017, 9.

Kee, Alistair. *Nietzsche against the Crucified*. London: SCM, 1999.

Klavan, Andrew. *The Great Good Thing: A Secular Jew Comes to Faith in Christ*. Nashville: Nelson, 2016.

Koch, Klaus. "Stages in the Canonization of the Book of Daniel." In *The Book of Daniel: Composition and Reception*, edited by John J. Collins and Peter W. Flint, 2:421–46. Leiden: Brill, 2002.

Lash, Nicholas. "Anselm Seeking." In *The Beginning and the End of 'Religion,'* 150–63.

———. *The Beginning and the End of 'Religion.'* Cambridge: Cambridge University Press, 1995.

———. "Creation, Courtesy, and Contemplation." In *The Beginning and the End of 'Religion,'* 164–82.

———. "On What Kinds of Things There Are." In *The Beginning and the End of 'Religion,'* 93–111.

Lawrence, D. H. "Why the Novel Matters." In *Selected Literary Criticism*, edited by Anthony Beal, 102–8. London: Heinemann, 1956.

Legaspi, Michael. *The Death of Scripture and the Rise of Biblical Studies*. OSHT. Oxford: Oxford University Press, 2010.

Lewis, C. Day. *The Eclogues, Georgics and Aeneid of Virgil*. London: Oxford University Press, 1966.

Lewis, C. S. *Collected Letters*. Vol. 3, *Narnia, Cambridge, and Joy, 1950–1963*. Edited by Walter Hooper. London: HarperCollins, 2006.

Loane, Helen A. "The *Sortes Vergilianae.*" *Classical Weekly* 21, no. 24 (1928): 185–89.

Louth, Andrew. *Discerning the Mystery: An Essay on the Nature of Theology.* Oxford: Clarendon, 1983.

Loveday, Simon. *The Bible for Grown-Ups: A New Look at the Good Book.* London: Icon, 2016.

Luz, Ulrich. *Matthew 21–28.* Hermeneia. Minneapolis: Fortress, 2005.

MacIntyre, Alasdair. *Three Rival Versions of Moral Enquiry.* London: Duckworth, 1990.

———. *Whose Justice? Which Rationality?* London: Duckworth, 1988.

Markus, R. A. *Saeculum: History and Society in the Theology of St. Augustine.* Cambridge: Cambridge University Press, 1970.

Martin, Dale B. *Pedagogy of the Bible: An Analysis and Proposal.* Louisville: Westminster John Knox, 2008.

Martínez, Florentino García, and Eibert J. C. Tigchelaar, eds. *The Dead Sea Scrolls Study Edition.* Vol. 1, *1Q1–4Q273.* Grand Rapids: Eerdmans, 1997.

Mencken, H. L. "Memorial Service." In *H. L. Mencken on Religion*, edited by S. T. Joshi, 293–97. Amherst, NY: Prometheus, 2002.

Moberly, R. W. L. *The Bible, Theology, and Faith: A Study of Abraham and Jesus.* CSCD. Cambridge: Cambridge University Press, 2000.

———. "Canon and Religious Truth: An Appraisal of *A New New Testament.*" In *When Texts Are Canonized*, edited by Timothy Lim, 108–35. Atlanta: SBL Press, 2017.

———. "How Can We Know the Truth? A Study of John 7:14–18." In *The Art of Reading Scripture*, edited by Ellen F. Davis and Richard B. Hays, 239–57. Grand Rapids: Eerdmans, 2003.

———. "Theological Interpretation, Presuppositions, and the Role of the Church: Bultmann and Augustine Revisited." *Journal of Theological Interpretation* 6, no. 1 (2012): 1–22.

———. *The Theology of the Book of Genesis.* OTT. New York: Cambridge University Press, 2009.

Moore, James R., ed. *Religion in Victorian Britain.* Vol. 3, *Sources.* Manchester, UK: Manchester University Press, 1988.

Mynors, R. A. B., ed. *P. Vergili Maronis Opera.* OCT. Oxford: Clarendon, 1969.

Newbigin, Lesslie. *The Gospel in a Pluralist Society.* London: SPCK, 1989.

Newsom, Carol A., with Brennan W. Breed. *Daniel.* OTL. Louisville: Westminster John Knox, 2014.

Numbers, Ronald L., ed. *Galileo Goes to Jail, and Other Myths about Science and Religion.* Cambridge, MA: Harvard University Press, 2009.

O'Neill, Onora. *A Question of Trust.* The BBC Reith Lectures 2002. Cambridge: Cambridge University Press, 2002.

Oremus.org. "The Form and Order of Service That Is to Be Performed and the Ceremonies That Are to Be Observed in The Coronation of Her Majesty Queen Elizabeth II in the Abbey Church of St. Peter, Westminster, on Tuesday, the Second Day of June, 1953." http://www.oremus.org /liturgy/coronation/cor1953b.html.

Phys.org. "Archaeologists Pinpoint the Date When Domesticated Camels Arrived in Israel." February 3, 2014. http://phys.org/news/2014-02 -archaeologists-date-domesticated-camels-israel.html.

Pritchard, James, ed. *Ancient Near Eastern Texts Relating to the Old Testament.* 3rd ed. Princeton: Princeton University Press, 1969.

Prudentius. *The Poems of Prudentius.* Vol. 2. Translated by Sister M. Clement Eagan, CCVI. FC. Washington, DC: Catholic University of America Press, 1962.

Räisänen, Heikki. "The Bible and the Traditions of the Nations: Isaac la Peyrère as a Precursor of Biblical Criticism." In *Marcion, Muhammad and the Mahatma,* 137–52. London: SCM, 1997.

Rorty, Richard. *Consequences of Pragmatism.* Minneapolis: University of Minnesota Press, 1982.

Ruden, Sarah. *The Aeneid / Vergil.* New Haven and London: Yale University Press, 2008.

Sandys-Wunsch, John, and Laurence Eldredge. "J. P. Gabler and the Distinction between Biblical and Dogmatic Theology: Translation, Commentary, and Discussion of His Originality." *Scottish Journal of Theology* 33 (1980): 133–58.

Sapir-Hen, Lidar, and Erez Ben-Yosef. "The Introduction of Domestic Camels to the Southern Levant: Evidence from the Aravah Valley." *Tel Aviv* 40 (2013): 277–85.

Sarna, Nahum. *The JPS Torah Commentary: Genesis.* Philadelphia and Jerusalem: Jewish Publication Society, 1989.

Satlow, Michael L. "Bad Prophecies: Canon and the Case of the Book of Daniel." In *When Texts Are Canonized,* edited by Timothy Lim, 63–81. Atlanta: SBL Press, 2017.

Schüssler Fiorenza, Elisabeth, ed. *Searching the Scriptures, Vol. 2: A Feminist Commentary*. London: SCM, 1995.

Shea, Victor, and William Whitla, eds. *Essays and Reviews: The 1860 Text and Its Reading*. Charlottesville and London: University Press of Virginia, 2000.

Ska, Jean Louis. "Questions of the 'History of Israel' in Recent Research." In *Hebrew Bible / Old Testament: The History of Its Interpretation*. Vol. III/2, *The Twentieth Century—From Modernism to Post-Modernism*, edited by Magne Sæbø, 391–432. Göttingen: Vandenhoeck & Ruprecht, 2015.

Smith, James K. A. *How (Not) to Be Secular: Reading Charles Taylor*. Grand Rapids: Eerdmans, 2014.

Smith, Jonathan Z. "Sacred Persistence: Toward a Redescription of Canon." In *Imagining Religion: From Babylon to Jonestown*, 36–52. Chicago and London: University of Chicago Press, 1982.

Smith-Christopher, Daniel L. "The Book of Daniel." In *The New Interpreter's Bible*, edited by Leander E. Keck, 7:17–152. Nashville: Abingdon, 1996.

Sommer, Benjamin D. *Revelation and Authority: Sinai in Jewish Scripture and Tradition*. New Haven and London: Yale University Press, 2015.

Spinoza, Benedict de. *Benedict de Spinoza: "A Theologico-Political Treatise" and "A Political Treatise."* Edited and translated by R. H. M. Elwes. New York: Dover, 1951.

Spufford, Francis. *Unapologetic: Why, Despite Everything, Christianity Can Still Make Surprising Emotional Sense*. London: Faber & Faber, 2012.

Stanford, Peter. "The Tablet Interview: Uncompromising Voice for Uncomfortable Truth." Interview with Amos Oz. *The Tablet*, October 8, 2016, 10–11.

Stegemann, Ekkehard W. "Coexistence and Transformation: Reading the Politics of Identity in Romans in an Imperial Context." In *Reading Paul in Context: Explorations in Identity Formation; Essays in Honour of William S. Campbell*, edited by Kathy Ehrensperger and J. Brian Tucker, 3–23. London: T&T Clark, 2010.

Stok, Fabio. "The Life of Vergil before Donatus." In *A Companion to Vergil's* Aeneid *and Its Tradition*, edited by Joseph Farrell and Michael C. J. Putnam, 107–20. Chichester, UK: Wiley-Blackwell, 2010.

Strawn, Brent. *The Old Testament Is Dying: A Diagnosis and Recommended Treatment*. Grand Rapids: Baker Academic, 2017.

Tarrant, R. J. "Aspects of Virgil's Reception in Antiquity." In *The Cambridge Companion to Virgil*, edited by Charles Martindale, 56–72. Cambridge: Cambridge University Press, 1997.

———. "Poetry and Power: Virgil's Poetry in Contemporary Context." In *The Cambridge Companion to Virgil*, edited by Charles Martindale, 169–87. Cambridge: Cambridge University Press, 1997.

Taussig, Hal, ed. *A New New Testament: A Bible for the 21st Century Combining Traditional and Newly Discovered Texts*. Boston and New York: Houghton Mifflin Harcourt, 2013.

Taylor, Charles. *A Secular Age*. Cambridge, MA: Belknap Press of Harvard University Press, 2005.

Turner, James. *Philology: The Forgotten Origins of the Modern Humanities*. Princeton and Oxford: Princeton University Press, 2014.

Vanhoozer, Kevin. "On Scripture." In *The Cambridge Companion to C. S. Lewis*, edited by Robert MacSwain and Michael Ward, 75–88. Cambridge: Cambridge University Press, 2010.

Vermes, G., trans. *The Dead Sea Scrolls in English*. 4th ed. Harmondsworth, UK: Penguin, 1995.

Viviano, Benedict, OP. "The Historical-Critical Method in Modern Biblical Studies: Yes or No?" In *Catholic Hermeneutics Today: Critical Essays*, 1–13. Eugene, OR: Cascade, 2014.

Wilford, John Noble. "Camels Had No Business in Genesis." *New York Times*, February 11, 2014, D3. http://www.nytimes.com/2014/02/11/science/camels-had-no-business-in-genesis.html.

Wills, Gary. "Vergil and St. Augustine." In *A Companion to Vergil's Aeneid and Its Tradition*, edited by Joseph Farrell and Michael C. J. Putnam, 123–32. Chichester, UK: Wiley-Blackwell, 2010.

Woods, Robert. *The Demography of Victorian England and Wales*. Cambridge: Cambridge University Press, 2000.

Wyhe, John van, and Mark J. Pallen. "The 'Annie Hypothesis': Did the Death of His Daughter Cause Darwin to 'Give Up Christianity'?" *Centaurus* 54, no. 2 (2012): 105–23.

Ziolkowski, Theodore. *Virgil and the Moderns*. Princeton: Princeton University Press, 1993.

Zonszein, Mairav. "Domesticated Camels Came to Israel in 930 B.C., Centuries Later Than Bible Says." *National Geographic*, February 10, 2014. http://news.nationalgeographic.com/news/2014/02/140210-domesticated-camels-israel-bible-archaeology-science/.

INDEX OF AUTHORS

INDEX OF SCRIPTURE AND OTHER ANCIENT SOURCES

INDEX OF SUBJECTS

2017. 12. 29   25.00 (16.50)